Introduction

Amish and Mennonite food is often thought of as good old-fashioned, stick-to-your-ribs comfort food. But beyond the delicious, hearty taste, the food seems to offer something to nourish the soul. The recipes, handed down through generations, come from a time when families were closely connected to their land, raising, growing, and harvesting everything they consumed. The dishes are a reflection of the Amish and Mennonite culture, highlighting their European and agricultural heritage and the strong bonds of family and community that are such an important part of Amish and Mennonite life. The food is grown out of hard work and is made with love. To understand what is so special about Amish and Mennonite food, it is helpful to know more about the culture.

A Very Brief History of Amish, Mennonites, and Anabaptism

The Amish and the Mennonites are part of a religious group whose members are found throughout the United States, Canada, and many other countries. The Mennonite church began in Switzerland in the early sixteenth century during the time following the Protestant Reformation of Martin Luther, maintaining two central beliefs. First, they rejected infant baptism, believing a Christian community should be made of adults who could knowingly and voluntarily confess their faith and choose to be baptized. Second, they believed the church should be a separate entity from the state.

In Amish communities, spring brings the arrival of "mud sales"—no further explanation needed as seen above. Occurring when fields are still too wet to till, "mud sales" are great social events for the Amish, other local farmers, and the plucky tourist or city dweller.

When members of this Swiss group confessed their faith and baptized each other, they earned the name Anabaptizers or re-baptizers. At the time, these beliefs and actions were extremely radical, and many Anabaptists were heavily persecuted and their leaders killed. When persecution in Europe became too great, many members fled to the New World. In 1683, German-speaking immigrants established a Mennonite community in Pennsylvania, and during the next several decades, Mennonites continued to move west, establishing a presence throughout the country. Those who remained in Europe moved into Prussia (Poland) and then to the south of Russia at the invitation of Catherine the Great. The many European wars of the 1800s and the Russian Revolution of the early 1900s caused many to move to the United States, Canada, and even South America. Non-resistance and pacifism are critical in Amish and Mennonites faith.

The Amish and Mennonites, although part of the same religious group, sometimes differ in their fundamental beliefs about dress, their connection to mainstream society, and other similar religious and cultural matters. The Old-Order Amish follow the most conservative teachings, striving to maintain a pure, simple lifestyle. They separate themselves from the rest of the world to strengthen their beliefs and values, living without creature comforts like electricity, running water, and cars.

The Amish choose to dress simply, in a manner they believe is called for in scripture. Women wear head coverings and do not cut their hair. All Amish clothing, both men's and women's, is made of solid colors and lacks adornments like buttons. This style of dress is meant to maintain simplicity and modesty in a world where glamour and immodesty can be highly emphasized.

Beyond their dress, the Amish are known for their policy of nonviolence and nonresistance, a belief that comes directly from the Biblical message to turn the other cheek. They also believe in community and communal support. The Amish feel it is their responsibility, and no one else's, to support and assist members of their faith. As a result, the Amish do not accept any aid or welfare from the government or other organizations, choosing instead to depend on those around them for aid.

While the Amish strictly adhere to and follow these beliefs, their practices are not typical of the larger, less-conservative segment of the Mennonite church. Most Mennonites have immersed themselves in modern society, living in houses with electricity and driving cars to and from work. What makes modern believers Mennonites is their continued adherence to the values of the Swiss reformers. Mennonites today still recognize the importance of maintaining a separation between church and state and believe that decisions about baptism, as well as church membership, should be made when adults.

Along with their religious beliefs, the Mennonites have maintained much of their European cultural heritage. Many Amish communities continue to speak a form of German most commonly known as Pennsylvania Dutch. But by far, the most well-known aspect of the heritage is the food. These dishes typically have a strong connection to the European countries in which group members lived. They were widely scattered, and their food is equally varied, reflecting culinary tastes from

countries such as Switzerland, Germany, Russia, Prussia, Hungary, and many more.

These recipes also demonstrate the agricultural heritage of the group. Most Amish and Mennonite families were farmers, and all of their food was produced from what they could raise and grow on the farm. Ingredients lists for the dishes in this book often call for garden produce, fresh meats, and dairy products. This close connection to the land and the ingredients seems to make these recipes that much more special. You can gain a sense of the hours of hard labor that went into growing and preparing the food and the satisfaction and accomplishment felt when sitting down at the table after a good day's work.

It is not unexpected to come across an unusual or surprising ingredient, as many recipes were developed with what was readily available. Substitutions and variations are typical; if one ingredient was not on hand, recipes were adapted to work with what was accessible at the time. For the most part, recipes were not written down, and there was no measuring involved. Cooks added ingredients as they saw fit until they were satisfied with the result, meaning each recipe in this book has a little something special added to it by each person who made it.

Beyond reflecting a European and agricultural heritage, Amish and Mennonite food highlights a community culture. Food is used to bring people together at events such as barn raisings or quilting

bees and to support relief efforts by organizations such as Mennonite Central Committee (MCC). Many of the recipes in this book were collected from relief sales held by MCC and were used to raise funds to support those in need around the world.

This book is a collection of favorite traditional recipes gathered from the Amish and Mennonite community, passed down from generation to generation, made with love, and meant to be shared. We hope they bring you comfort and fond memories as you enjoy them with your family and friends.

—Enjoy!

How This Book Came To Be

The recipes in our three previous Amish and Mennonite cookbooks (Treasured Mennonite Recipes, More Treasured Mennonite Recipes, and Treasured Amish & Mennonite Recipes) were collected beginning in 1992 from Mennonite and Amish homes across North America. The first book celebrated the success of the "relief sale" tradition— community fundraisers that Mennonite Central Committee (MCC) has held for more than 40 years.

Several years ago, I went through these recipes, updating as needed, and whittling down or expanding the number of selections (I found we had far too many recipes for certain foods and were missing a few common Amish-Mennonite dishes).

For this edition, we decided on this page size and hardcover spiral binding to make the book very reader- and cook-friendly. I hope you will find it to be a cookbook you use often, and one that inspires you both creatively and in your spirit.

Charitable Giving

As a former elementary school teacher, I have a special place in my heart for helping children wherever they may live. MCC projects are well-managed and practical ways to help others.

Mennonite Central Committee is probably the most common and popular donation choice for Amish and Mennonite church members of all types, from conservative to modern.

In addition to giving copies of this book to MCC for use in fundraising, 10% of the sales of this book by the publisher are donated to MCC and designated for projects to relieve poverty, develop food security and agricultural projects, and to promote self-sufficiency in lower income countries.

The three previous cookbooks I published have generated more than $175,000 in income for Mennonite Central Committee.

Thanks for buying the book! I hope you have as much fun reading and cooking for your family as I did creating it.

Contents

 Before You Begin

Before you select a recipe and start cooking, here are some things you might need to know.

Salad dressing. *Throughout this book, you might see "salad dressing" appear on the ingredients lists. This term does not refer to French, Honey Dijon, or your own favorite salad dressing, but rather to Miracle Whip salad dressing or your favorite equivalent brand. Use this or mayonnaise when the ingredients list calls for salad dressing.*

Potato water. *Potato water refers to water in which potatoes have been boiled. After boiling, some of the starch from the potatoes is left behind in the water. This water is often called for in bread recipes because it makes the bread incredibly moist. It can also replace milk in a bread recipe. Make potato water by boiling several peeled and cubed potatoes for 20 minutes. Let the water temperature come down before you use it.*

Candy stages. *Candy recipes might refer to candy syrup that has reached the thread, soft ball, or hard ball stage. Syrup that has reached the thread stage has a temperature between 230°F and 235°F and, when dropped into cold water, will form thin threads. Syrup that has reached the soft ball stage has a temperature of between 235°F and 240°F and, when dropped into cold water, will form a ball that is soft and malleable to the touch, able to be flattened a few moments after it has been removed from the water. Syrup that has reached the hard ball stage has a temperature between 250°F and 265°F and, when dropped into cold water, will form a hard ball that won't flatten, although you should be able to change its shape slightly by squeezing it.*

Drinks and Appetizers

Grape Juice

- 1 cup grapes, washed and stemmed
- ¾ cup sugar

Put the grapes into a sterile 1-quart sealer. Add the sugar and slowly fill with boiling water (jars crack easily if water is poured too fast). Seal and store. In a month, you can pour off a lovely juice to serve as it is or mix it with lemon and ginger ale to taste.

Juice

Always use real juice for these recipes, not juice substitutes. You'll enjoy the flavor that much more.

Photo courtesy of The Gray Boxwood, www.thegrayboxwood.com

 Our duty is not to see through one another but to see one another through.

Amish and Mennonite Bookshelf

Those familiar with Amish and Mennonite culture can often tell a lot about a person or church by their choice in Bible versions or hymnbooks. Amish use the Martin Luther German translation of the Bible, or if English, the Kings James Bible. They use a unique German hymnal—the Ausbund—with hymns that, to non-Amish, sound very slow and often mournful.

Due to the wide range of Mennonites, the range of Bible and hymnbook choices is too long to include here, although the most conservative Mennonites still read the King James Bible exclusively.

Raspberry Juice

- 4 quarts raspberries
- Vinegar
- Sugar

Put the raspberries in a crock and cover with vinegar. Let stand in a cool place for 24 hours. Heat to boiling point and strain. Add 1 cup sugar to each cup of juice. Boil 15 minutes and seal in sterile jars.

Rhubarb Juice

Boil rhubarb in the water until very soft. Strain. Stir sugar into strained juice and bring to a boil. Pour into hot sterilized jars and seal, or cool and freeze. Make punch, if desired, by adding 2 large bottles lemon-lime soda or ginger ale and 1 large can (12 ounces) frozen orange juice, thawed.

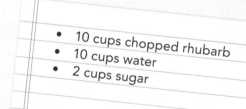

- 10 cups chopped rhubarb
- 10 cups water
- 2 cups sugar

Tip: To prevent cut fruits from discoloring before preserving, place them in a gallon of water mixed with 3 tablespoons of lemon juice. Drain well before canning.

Tomato Juice

- 11 quarts tomatoes
- 1 stalk celery
- 3 onions
- ½ cup sugar
- 2 tablespoons salt
- 2 tablespoons vinegar

Cut tomatoes coarsely. Boil with celery and onions for 30 minutes and strain. Bring juice to a boil and add sugar, salt, and vinegar. Boil 5 minutes and seal.

Friendship Tea

- 3 packages Tang
- ⅓ cup instant tea
- 1 package lemonade mix
- ½ cup sugar
- 1 teaspoon cloves
- 1 teaspoon cinnamon (ground)

Mix. To use, put 2–3 teaspoons in a cup and fill with boiling water.

 Tip: Freeze leftover tea in ice cube trays, and add the cubes to your next glass of iced tea.

Mint Tea

- 1 tea bag (or more for stronger flavor)
- 6 stems mint, slightly crushed
- Dash cayenne pepper
- 2 cups boiling water
- 1 cup sugar
- ½ cup lemon juice

Steep the tea bag and mint in boiling water with cayenne pepper. Strain. Add the sugar and lemon juice. Refrigerate. Dilute with water when ready to serve.

 Tip: To keep iced tea from clouding over, keep the tea at room temperature. When it's time to serve, just pour it over ice cubes.

Swiss Tea

- ½ cup green tea (preferably Tender Leaf tea)
- 2 sticks cinnamon, broken into pieces
- ½ teaspoon (or big pinch) saffron
- 1½ cups sugar (more or less to taste)
- 1 quart boiling water

Add tea, cinnamon, and saffron to 1 quart boiling water. Simmer 15–20 minutes. Strain. Add enough hot water to make 1 gallon tea. Stir in the sugar until dissolved.

Tip: You'll get a tastier cup of tea if you brew it in a clean china or earthenware pot, using fresh, cold water that's been brought quickly to a boil.

Hot Spiced Apple Cider

- 4 teaspoons whole cloves
- 4 teaspoons whole allspice
- 4 cinnamon sticks
- 2 gallons apple cider
- ½–1 cup brown sugar (more or less to taste)

Tie spices together in cheesecloth. Add spice bag to cider and heat to desired temperature (do not boil). Serve hot. Add ½–1 cup brown sugar if cider is too tart.

Photo courtesy of The Gray Boxwood, www.thegrayboxwood.com

Quick Root Beer

- 2 cups white sugar
- 1 gallon lukewarm water
- 4 teaspoons root beer extract
- 1 teaspoon dry yeast

Use some hot water to dissolve sugar. Mix all ingredients together. Put in jars. Cover and set in sun for 4 hours. Chill before serving. Ready to serve the next day. No need to bottle. From *Amish Cooking*, published by Pathway Publishers Corporation.

 ## Living the Simple Life

Thriftiness is part of Amish culture. With large families, the Amish have learned to be frugal and to make the most out of the household items they have. Whether it's food, clothing, furniture, or bedding, Amish culture teaches a person not to be wasteful.

Fruit Punch

Serves 35

- 1½ quarts pineapple juice
- 1 6-ounce can frozen lemonade
- 1 12-ounce can frozen orange juice
- 1 quart cranberry juice
- 1½ quarts cold water
- 1 cup sugar
- Half of a 3-ounce package cherry gelatin dissolved in 1 cup boiling water
- 1 quart ginger ale or lemon-lime soda
- Orange or lemon sherbet **(optional)**

Mix all together. At serving time, add 1 quart ginger ale or lemon-lime soda. Add orange or lemon sherbet if desired.

 Tip: To keep the flavor fresh, store tea bags and loose tea in an airtight tin can.

Orange Julius

- 1 6-ounce can frozen orange juice
- 1 cup milk
- 1 cup water
- ¼ cup sugar
- 1 teaspoon vanilla
- 10–12 ice cubes

Combine all ingredients in a blender. Blend until smooth. Serve at once.

Tip: When squeezing your own orange juice, press the orange and roll it gently on the table or countertop. You'll get more juice.

Pink Lassies

- 2 cups cranberry juice
- ½ cup orange juice
- 2 cups vanilla ice cream, softened

Combine all ingredients in a blender. Blend until smooth. Serve in a tall glass with a straw.

Living the Simple Life

The Amish take part in many volunteer activities. In Lancaster County, Pennsylvania, many Amish men belong to the volunteer fire department. Many Amish women make quilts and other items to sell at benefit auctions, which help people in other parts of the world.

Apple Dip

- 8 ounces cream cheese, softened
- ¾ cup brown sugar
- ¼ cup granulated sugar
- 2 teaspoons vanilla

Mix all ingredients well to blend. Serve with raw apple slices.

Living the Simple Life

Frugal by nature, the Amish prepare home-cooked meals with fresh or canned food grown in their own gardens.

Fancy Sliced Tomatoes

- 3 fresh tomatoes (unpeeled), sliced
- 1 onion, thinly sliced
- Fresh basil leaves, minced
- 1 teaspoon olive oil
- 1 teaspoon vinegar of choice
- 1 teaspoon sugar
- Salt and pepper to taste

Combine sugar, vinegar, and olive oil and set aside. In a nice serving bowl, put a layer of tomatoes and onions, season with salt, pepper, and a sprinkle of basil. Pour several spoonfuls of oil and vinegar mixture over tomatoes and onions. Repeat layers and seasonings. Cucumbers may be added to the layers if desired.

 Whatever you fill your mind with fills your heart, and whatever fills your heart comes out of your mouth.

" *Enjoy today, it won't come back.* "

Amish-Style Deviled Eggs

- 12 eggs
- 2 tablespoons mayonnaise
- 1 heaping tablespoon yellow mustard
- 4 ounces chopped olives
- Dash salt and pepper

Bring a large pan of water to a boil, then turn off heat. Prick the end of the shell of each egg and drop gently into the hot water. Cover and let sit for 20 minutes. Pour out water. Rinse eggs in cold water. Peel. Halve eggs and remove yolks. Place in medium bowl and mash. Mix in mayonnaise, mustard, olives, salt, and pepper. Stuff eggs with mixture.

Red Beet Eggs

Tip: Wash a foam egg carton and use it as a carrying case for deviled eggs.

- 1 15-ounce can beets
- 1 onion, thinly sliced
- 12 hard-boiled eggs, shelled and left whole
- ¼ cup sugar
- ½ cup vinegar

Drain liquid from the beets into saucepan. Place beets, onion, and eggs in a large glass bowl.

Pour sugar and vinegar into the saucepan with the beet liquid and bring the mixture to a boil. Reduce the heat to low and let the mixture simmer for 15 minutes.

Pour the beet juice mixture over the beets, eggs, and onion. Seal the bowl and refrigerate. Refrigerate for at least 48 hours; the longer they are allowed to sit the better they will taste.

Cheese Ball

- 2 8-ounce packages cream cheese, softened
- 1 8-ounce can crushed pineapple, drained
- ¼ cup green pepper, chopped
- ¼ cup onion, chopped
- ¼ teaspoon garlic powder
- Pinch of salt
- ¼ teaspoon chives and/or parsley (*(optional)*)
- Pecans, chopped

Mix all ingredients except pecans together with mixer. Roll into a ball. Roll ball into chopped pecans until covered. Alternatively, roll ball in additional chopped chives or parsley. Refrigerate until ready to serve.

Snack Crackers or Croutons

Combine all ingredients except crackers. Mix well. Pour over crackers to coat. Place on baking pans and bake for 15–20 minutes at 250°F. Cool. Store in an airtight container. Use as a snack or as croutons on a salad.

- 1 16-ounce bag oyster crackers
- 1 package ranch dressing mix
- 1 teaspoon garlic powder
- 1 teaspoon onion powder
- 1 teaspoon dill weed
- 1 teaspoon parsley flakes
- ½ cup oil

Ham Balls

- 1–1½ pounds ground ham
- 1–1½ pounds ground beef
- 2 eggs, beaten
- 2 cups bread crumbs
- 1 cup milk
- Salt and pepper to taste

Sauce:

- 1½ cups brown sugar
- 1 tablespoon dry mustard
- ½ cup vinegar
- ½ cup water

Mix together ingredients for ham balls. Form into about 25 small balls. Place in a roaster. Mix together sauce ingredients. Pour over ham balls. Cover and bake at 350°F for 2 hours.

Soups, Salads, and Dressings

Broccoli-Cauliflower-Cheese Soup

- 3 chicken bouillon cubes
- 3 cups water
- ½ cup diced celery
- ½ cup diced green pepper
- ½ cup diced carrots
- ¼ cup diced onion
- 1 cup cauliflower, cut into flowerets
- 1 cup broccoli, cut up
- 6 cups milk
- ½ cup butter, melted
- ½ cup flour
- 1 cup cubed Velveeta cheese

Dissolve bouillon cubes in water in soup kettle. Add celery, green pepper, carrots, and onion. Cook until partly tender. Add cauliflower and broccoli. Cook until all vegetables are tender. Add milk to soup. Heat, but do not boil.

Blend together butter and flour in separate saucepan. Cook until frothy but not browned. Remove from heat and blend with small amount of the soup broth to thin mixture. Add to soup kettle. Stir until well blended. Add cheese. Heat soup gently and stir to prevent sticking until cheese melts. Do not let soup boil.

Butter Soup with Angel Food Dumplings

- 6 cups water
- 1 onion, diced
- 6 medium potatoes, diced
- 2 bay leaves
- 4 peppercorns
- 5 whole cloves

Dumplings:
- 1 cup all-purpose flour
- 2½ teaspoons baking powder
- ¼ teaspoon salt
- ⅓ cup milk
- 1 egg

Bring water to a boil, add onion and potatoes, and simmer 20 minutes. Add all the spices wrapped in a cheesecloth. Let simmer another 20 minutes. Stir together dry ingredients for dumplings. Beat egg and add milk. Add to dry ingredients. Drop by spoonfuls into boiling soup. Let rise until puffed (about 5 minutes) Cover and cook gently for about 15 minutes. Ladle into bowls and top with a dollop of butter and some fresh cream.

Cheese Soup

- 2 medium carrots
- 2 stalks celery
- 1 small onion
- 2 cups water
- 2 cups chicken broth
- 2 cups milk
- ¼ cup flour
- 2½ cups cheddar or Velveeta cheese, or some of each

Cut vegetables to go in blender, add water and process until ground. Pour in saucepan, add chicken broth, cover, and cook until tender. Put milk, flour, and cheese into blender; blend until smooth. Pour into hot vegetable mixture and stir until thickened.

Chicken Corn Soup

Serves 10–12

- 1 whole chicken
- 2 large carrots, sliced
- 1 medium onion, chopped
- 3 celery stalks, sliced
- 2 tablespoons parsley
- 1 10-ounce package frozen corn
- 1 package wide egg noodles
- 1 teaspoon salt
- ½ teaspoon black pepper
- Pinch of saffron
- 3 hard-boiled eggs, chopped

Place chicken in enough water to cover, and cook until tender. Remove meat from bones, chop, and return to pot with water. Add remaining ingredients (except eggs, noodles, and parsley) with more water if needed. Bring to a boil. Reduce heat to low and simmer for 30 minutes. Watch carefully so that soup does not scorch. Add noodles and parsley, bring back to boil, and simmer for 10 minutes. Remove from heat. Stir in chopped eggs and serve. Add additional water or broth if needed for desired consistency.

Great on a chilly day!

Chili Soup

- 1 pound ground beef
- 1 medium onion, roughly chopped
- 30 ounces red kidney beans
- 25 ounces tomato juice
- ½ teaspoon salt
- ½ teaspoon cinnamon
- 1 tablespoon chili powder
- ¼ teaspoon pepper

Brown ground beef and onion in a large pot. Drain off excess grease and add remaining ingredients. Simmer together for 20 minutes. Doubling or even tripling the size of the recipe works well if you have a large crowd to serve.

Corn Chowder

- 5 slices bacon, crumbled
- 1 medium onion, chopped
- 2 diced potatoes
- ½ cup water
- 1–2 cups corn
- 2 cups milk
- 1 teaspoon salt
- Dash of pepper

Brown bacon and onion in a large skillet. Add potatoes and water and cook until potatoes are tender. Add remaining ingredients, heat, and serve.

An excellent side for seafood dishes

Tip: Soup too thin? Add mashed potatoes or instant rice, stirring until you get the desired consistency.

Corn Soup with Rivels

- 3 cups fresh or canned corn
- 2 quarts water
- 1 cup whole milk
- 1⅓ cups flour
- 1 egg
- 3 tablespoons butter
- 1½ teaspoons salt
- Parsley

Tip: When making stock, never allow the liquid to boil. Boiling will make the stock cloudy.

Cook corn in water for 10 minutes. Make a batter by mixing egg, flour, and milk together. Pour this batter through a colander, letting it drop into the boiling corn (this forms the rivels). Add butter and salt. Cook slowly in a covered pan for 3 minutes. Garnish with chopped parsley. Soup should be eaten immediately after rivels are cooked.

Dutch Potato Soup

This recipe serves four or two if they are farmers!

- 2 cups diced potatoes
- ½ cup diced onion ((*optional*))
- 3 cups water
- 1 teaspoon salt
- 1 cup chopped celery
- ½ cup grated carrot
- 1 quart milk
- 2 tablespoons butter
- 3 hard-boiled eggs, chopped
- 1 tablespoon chopped fresh parsley

Bring potatoes, onion, water, and salt to a boil. Simmer briefly. Add celery and carrot when potatoes are partially cooked. Heat milk in separate saucepan. Add to soup mixture when potatoes are soft. Stir in butter, eggs, and parsley just before serving.

Green Bean Soup

Serves 8
- 1½–2 pounds ham bones and meat
- 4–5 sprigs summer savory
- 2 cups diced potatoes
- 4 cups cut green beans
- 1 teaspoon salt
- 2 tablespoons ham-flavored soup base
- 2 cups sour cream

Place ham bones and summer savory in cooking pot. Cover with water and cook about 2 hours. Remove ham from bones. Chop meat and return to pot. Add potatoes, beans, salt, and ham base. Cook until vegetables are tender. Stir in sour cream just before serving.

Household Hint

When cooking dry beans, a little baking soda will keep them from getting mushy.

Hamburger Soup

- 1 pound ground beef
- 1 medium onion, chopped
- 4 carrots, chopped
- 3 celery stalks, chopped
- 16 ounces tomato sauce
- 1 quart tomato juice
- 1 teaspoon parsley flakes
- ⅛ teaspoon garlic powder
- 1 teaspoon dried basil
- ¼ teaspoon marjoram
- 1 tablespoon brown sugar
- ½ teaspoon Italian seasoning
- Long spaghetti noodles, broken into pieces (as much as desired)
- Dash of red pepper

Brown ground beef and onion, drain off any excess grease, set aside. Put chopped vegetables in a large pot, cover with about 2 inches of water, and cook 10 minutes. Add ground beef and the rest of the ingredients except the spaghetti. Simmer until vegetables are done. Before serving, add the broken spaghetti. Simmer until soft. If soup is too thick, add water. This recipe freezes well. When soup is reheated, it tends to get thick. Add more tomato juice or water to thin as desired. More spices may also be added.

Meatball Soup

- 1 medium onion, sliced
- 2 stalks celery, sliced
- 1 grated carrot
- 4 potatoes, peeled and cubed
- 1 bay leaf
- Salt and pepper
- 2½ quarts water
- ½ cup sour cream

Meatballs:
- 1 pound ground beef
- 1 egg
- 1 small onion, chopped
- 1 small potato, grated
- Salt, pepper, and chopped parsley

Cook vegetables, bay leaf, and seasonings in water in large stock pot. Cook until vegetables just begin to get tender. Mix ingredients for meatballs. Form into balls and drop into soup. Continue boiling for 20 minutes. Reduce heat to a simmer. Remove from heat and stir in sour cream when ready to serve.

Oyster Soup

For each bowl of soup, heat 1½ cups milk. When hot, add 3–4 oysters (or more) to each bowl. Season with the salt, pepper, and butter. Heat until oysters are hot and curl a bit.

- 1½ cups milk
- 3 or 4 oysters
- Salt, pepper, and butter to taste

Photo courtesy of Discover Lancaster, www.discoverlancaster.com

Living the Simple Life

Because the Amish have no electric dryers, they hang their laundry outside to dry. When you have the time and the weather is nice, try hanging your laundry outside to dry. You'll not only be saving energy, but the fresh, clean smell will relax your senses.

> *It takes both sunny and rainy days to make a life complete.*

Pluma Moos

Makes 1 gallon
- 1½ cups dried prunes
- 1½ cups dried apricots
- 1½ cups raisins
- 1 cinnamon stick
- 4 quarts water
- 1 cup sugar (or less)
- ¼–½ cup flour
- ½ cup cream
- ¾ cup milk

Soak dried fruits and cinnamon stick overnight in the water. The next morning, cook fruit in soaking water until soft (simmering 30 minutes to 1 hour). Mix together sugar, flour, cream, and milk to form a paste. Very slowly add to the hot fruit. Simmer 10 minutes more or until thickened. (Mixture will thicken more as it cools.) Cool. If you do not want a creamy moos, substitute same amount of water for the cream and milk.

Potato Chowder

- 2 cups potatoes, diced
- ½ cup carrots, diced
- ½ cup celery, diced
- ¼ cup onion, diced
- 2 cups water
- 1 cup ham, diced

Base:
- ¼ cup butter
- ¼ cup flour
- 2 cups milk
- 2 cups grated cheddar cheese

Cook vegetables until tender. Add diced ham. In another pot, heat butter, milk, and flour together until thickened. Add 2 cups grated cheese. Add to the vegetable mixture and serve.

Tip: If the stew or soup you're preparing seems too salty, add sugar or a few slices of raw potato. (Discard the potato slices before serving.)

Smoked Sausage Potato Soup

Serves 4–6
- 4 large potatoes, peeled
- 1 pound smoked sausage
- 1 tablespoon onion, finely chopped ((optional))
- ¼ teaspoon salt
- Milk
- Parsley

Cut sausage in ¼–inch pieces. Place in 3-quart pan with 2 inches water. Cube potatoes. Add to pan with sausage. Add onion and salt. Cover and bring to a boil. Cook over medium heat, stirring frequently to prevent sticking and burning bottom of pan. Cook 20–30 minutes until potatoes are soft. Cover with milk. Add a few sprinkles of dried or freshly chopped parsley if desired. Cover and let stand 5 minutes. It should be very thick.

Tomato Soup

 Try this with a grilled cheese sandwich!

- 1 medium onion, chopped
- 2 tablespoons butter
- 2 cans diced tomatoes, undrained
- 2 cans tomato soup, undiluted
- 1½ cups milk
- 1 teaspoon sugar
- ⅛ teaspoon garlic powder
- 1 teaspoon basil
- ½ teaspoon paprika
- 1 8-ounce package of cream cheese

Sauté onion in butter. Stir in tomatoes, soup, sugar, seasonings, and milk. Bring to a boil, reduce heat, cover, and simmer for 10 minutes. Stir in cream cheese until melted.

Tip: To keep milk from curdling when you prepare tomato soup, add the soup stock to the milk instead of the milk to the stock.

Vegetable, Beef, and Barley Soup

- 1 pound ground beef
- 2 medium onions, chopped
- 2 cups tomato juice
- ½ cup barley
- 3 carrots, diced
- 3 potatoes, diced
- 3 celery stalks, chopped
- 1 quart of water
- 1 teaspoon salt
- ¼ teaspoon pepper
- 1 teaspoon chili powder

Tip: The vitamin-rich water made when cooking vegetables can be frozen and used later for making a soup base.

Brown ground beef and onions. Drain off excess grease and set aside. Put barley, carrots, potatoes, celery, and seasonings in a large cooking pot. Cover with water and bring to a boil, turn down to simmer, and let cook for 30–40 minutes until vegetables are tender. Add tomato juice and meat mixture to vegetables and serve piping hot.

Wild Rice Soup with Chicken Dumplings

- 1 cup wild rice
- ¼ cup butter
- 2 cups finely diced carrots
- 2 cups finely diced celery
- 1 large onion, finely diced
- ⅓ cup oil
- ½ cup flour
- 3 cups cream or whole milk
- 5 cups chicken stock
- Salt and pepper to taste

Dumplings:
- 1 cup ground chicken pieces
- 1–2 eggs
- Salt and pepper

Precook the wild rice (it will take about an hour). Set aside. Melt butter in a heavy frying pan. Add carrots, celery, and onion. Sauté. Set aside. Make a white sauce with the oil, flour, and cream in a large stock pot. Add the chicken stock. Whisk until smooth. Add sautéed vegetables. Cook until vegetables are tender (about 15 minutes).

Stir soup and watch it carefully so it doesn't burn. Season to taste. Add reserved wild rice and simmer a few minutes more. Make dumpling mixture by using a blender to blend chicken until very fine. Add eggs and seasonings. Drop dumpling mixture by teaspoons into the soup shortly before serving. Simmer a few minutes until dumplings cook through.

Tip: If the rice you're cooking has burned slightly, you can remove the burned flavor by adding a heel from a loaf of fresh white bread and covering the pot for a few minutes.

Apple Salad

- Apples, chopped and sugared
- 1 egg, beaten
- 1 tablespoon flour
- 1 teaspoon vinegar
- ½ cup water
- ½ cup sugar
- 1 tablespoon butter
- Pinch of salt
- 1 cup whipped topping
- Sliced bananas, nuts, and marshmallows *(optional)*

Living the Simple Life

At barn raisings there's always more than enough help to get the job done. Even for things like preparing meals, cleaning the house, and doing outside chores, everyone chips in.

Boil all ingredients together, except apples, bananas, nuts, marshmallows, and whipped topping, until thickened. Cool, and add 1 cup whipped topping. Pour over apples that have been chopped and sugared. Add sliced bananas, nuts, and marshmallows as desired. Do not prepare far in advance as apples will become brown and mushy.

Tasty Apple Salad

- 2 cups diced apples
- Orange or pineapple juice (enough to cover apples)
- 2 cups diced celery
- 2 cups diced carrots
- 2 cups raisins
- 1 cup unsalted dry-roasted peanuts (broken into halves)
- 1 cup unsalted sunflower seeds
- Yogurt (plain or vanilla-flavored)

Dice apples directly into enough fruit juice to cover them. Let sit while dicing, measuring, and preparing remaining salad ingredients. Drain juice from apples. Combine with remaining ingredients, using enough yogurt to form a dressing.

Living the Simple Life

Amish attitudes toward money are based on Biblical principles. Saving is encouraged; frivolous spending and coveting are not. The Amish stay out of debt, give generously, and make investments in keeping with their values. Amish businesses thrive when others fail because the goal is to make a living, not make a killing.

Cranberry Fruit Medley

Makes 6 servings

- 2 cups fresh cranberries
- 2 medium-large apples, cored, but not peeled
- 2 medium-large bananas
- ¾ cup granulated sugar
- 2 cups miniature marshmallows **(optional)**
- 1 cup whipped topping **(optional)**

Coarsely chop cranberries and apples. Dice bananas and add to cranberry-apple mixture along with sugar. Stir well. Cover tightly and place in refrigerator for at least 3 hours or overnight to blend flavors. Add 2 cups miniature marshmallows with the fruit and stir in 1 cup whipped topping if desired.

Cranberry Salad

- 1 1-pound package cranberries
- 4 apples
- 2 chopped oranges or ½ cup crushed pineapple
- ½ cup nuts
- 2 cups sugar
- 3 packages raspberry gelatin
- 3 cups hot water
- 3 cups cold water

Wash and grind cranberries in food chopper. Pare and core apples and chop or grind. Add chopped oranges or pineapple, nuts, and sugar. Dissolve gelatin in hot water. Add cold water. When cool and beginning to congeal, add fruit salad mixture.

Broccoli Delight Salad

Serves 6
- 1 large bunch fresh broccoli, cut into pieces (4–5 cups)
- 1 cup raisins
- ¼ cup diced red onion *(optional)*
- 10 bacon strips, fried and crumbled
- 1 cup sunflower seeds

Dressing:
- 3–4 tablespoons sugar
- ½ cup light mayonnaise
- 1 tablespoon vinegar

Put washed and drained broccoli in large glass bowl. Add raisins, onion, bacon, and sunflower seeds. Mix dressing ingredients. Pour over salad. Chill before serving if desired.

Creamy Cabbage Slaw

Mix dressing ingredients and refrigerate overnight. Just before serving, add to cabbage, carrots, and eggs.

Perfect for Picnics

- 2 hard-boiled eggs, diced
- ¼ cup finely grated carrots
- 3 cups shredded cabbage

Dressing:
- 1 cup Miracle Whip
- ¼ cup half-and-half
- 1 tablespoon sugar
- 2 tablespoons vinegar
- ½ teaspoon salt
- ¼ teaspoon pepper

Creamy Cole Slaw Dressing

- 1 cup mayonnaise
- 1 cup cream (sweet or sour)
- ½ cup sugar
- ½ cup vinegar
- Salt to taste

Mix all ingredients together well. Recipe makes enough dressing for 1 medium head cabbage.

> "*A heart touched by grace brings joy to the face.*"

Emma's Bean Salad

- ½–1 cup sugar
- ½ cup lemon juice
- 1 small can kidney beans, drained
- 1 small can lima beans, drained
- 1 small can yellow beans, drained
- 1 small can green beans, drained
- 1½ cups chopped onion
- ½ cup chopped celery
- ½ cup chopped green pepper

Bring sugar and lemon juice to a boil. Remove from heat and cool slightly. Mix together remaining ingredients. Pour dressing over top. Toss well to coat all ingredients with dressing. Refrigerate overnight or longer.

Old-Fashioned Bean Salad

- 1 quart plain canned green and yellow beans
- 1 onion, chopped
- 1 teaspoon vinegar
- 1 teaspoon sugar
- Salt and pepper
- ¾ cup sour cream
- 2 hard-boiled eggs, chopped

Mix all ingredients except sour cream and eggs and let stand 2–3 hours. At serving time, add sour cream and eggs.

Faith and Resilience

Living simply does not mean the absence of challenge and danger. A common verse among Amish and Mennonite people reminds that ultimately faith is in God and not money or other externals.

"Therefore I tell you, do not worry about your life, what you will eat or drink; or about your body, what you will wear. Is not life more than food, and the body more than clothes? Look at the birds of the air; they do not sow or reap or store away in barns, and yet your heavenly Father feeds them. Are you not much more valuable than they? Can any one of you by worrying add a single hour to your life?" - **Matthew 6:25–27**

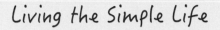

Yellow Bean Salad

- 1 quart yellow beans, cooked
- ½ onion, chopped
- 2 hard-boiled eggs, chopped
- Salt and pepper to taste

Dressing:
- 1 teaspoon vinegar
- 1 teaspoon sugar
- ¾ cup sour cream

Combine the beans, onion, eggs, and salt and pepper. Combine the ingredients for the dressing and pour over bean mixture.

Living the Simple Life

The Amish do not use credit cards or loans outside of their community if at all possible. Debt is considered dangerous as it may force the Amish to go against their beliefs in order to pay their creditors. Debt is discouraged and business partnerships with others outside their faiths is often prohibited, citing 2 Corinthians 6:14, "Be ye not yoked together with unbelievers."

Potato and Macaroni Salad

- 12 cups shredded potatoes, cooked
- 1 medium onion, chopped
- ¾ cup chopped celery
- 12 hard-boiled eggs
- 3 cups cooked macaroni or 1½ cups dried
- 1 cup shredded carrots

Dressing:
- 3 cups mayonnaise
- ¼ cup vinegar
- 2 tablespoons salt
- 6 tablespoons prepared mustard
- 1½ cups sugar
- 1¼ cups milk

Combine potatoes, macaroni, eggs, and vegetables. In a separate bowl, combine dressing ingredients. Pour over potato and macaroni mixture. Let set overnight in the refrigerator.

Tip: When boiling water for spaghetti or macaroni, add a teaspoon or so of cooking oil. The pasta won't stick together (or to the pot), and you needn't stir it constantly.

Hot Potato Salad

Serves 6

- 4 cups hot, diced potatoes
- 1 cup chopped celery
- 1 teaspoon chopped parsley
- 1 onion, chopped
- ½ teaspoon pepper
- 2 tablespoons salad oil or lard
- 1½ teaspoons salt
- 1 tablespoon flour
- ⅓ cup vinegar
- ⅓ cup sugar
- ⅔ cup water
- Pepper and paprika to taste

Fry chopped onion in hot lard or oil until light brown. Add flour and blend. Add salt, sugar, vinegar, and water. Bring to a boil, stirring constantly. Pour dressing over the potatoes. Mix in celery and parsley. Sprinkle with pepper and paprika and serve hot.

Raw Cauliflower and Broccoli Salad

- 2 cups broccoli, broken into small pieces
- 2 cups cauliflower, broken into small pieces
- 1 cup frozen peas, thawed
- ½ cup chopped onion

Dressing:

- 3 tablespoons lemon juice
- 3 tablespoons vinegar
- 1 teaspoon salt
- ½ teaspoon sugar
- ¼ teaspoon pepper

Combine salad ingredients. Combine dressing ingredients. Pour dressing over salad. Let marinate in refrigerator at least 1 hour (preferably overnight). Stir well before serving.

Salad of Greens

- 4 cups greens (dandelion, endive, spinach, or other greens of choice)
- 2–3 hard-boiled eggs

Dressing:
- 3 bacon slices
- 2 tablespoons flour
- 2–4 tablespoons sugar
- ¼ cup vinegar
- ½–¾ cup cream (milk or water can also be used)

Prepare dressing by cutting bacon into pieces and frying. Blend flour into hot bacon. Reduce heat and add sugar, vinegar, and cream. Bring dressing to a boil. Toss with greens and eggs, or toss with greens and shred egg over top to garnish. Serve at once. Do not allow to fully wilt.

Tip: A way to make lettuce or celery crisp again is to place it in a pot of cold water with slices of raw potato.

Fresh Spinach Salad

- 10–12 ounces fresh baby spinach
- 2 hard-boiled eggs, chopped or sliced
- 4 cooked bacon strips, crumbled
- 2 or 3 green onions, sliced

Dressing:
- ¼ cup red wine vinegar
- ¼ cup oil
- 1 teaspoon salt
- ¼ teaspoon black pepper
- 2 tablespoons sugar
- ½ teaspoon oregano

Remove the stems from the spinach and wash, drain, and thoroughly pat dry. Place in a large mixing bowl and set aside. Combine dressing ingredients in a container with a tight lid and shake well. Add eggs, onion, and bacon to spinach right before serving and top with dressing.

Tip: When dressing a salad with vinegar and oil, remember to pour the vinegar first. If you pour the oil first, the vinegar won't stick to the greens.

Dandelion Salad

- Young, tender dandelion greens
- 4 thick slices cooked bacon, crumbled
- ½ cup cream
- 2 tablespoons butter
- 2 eggs
- 1 teaspoon salt
- 1 tablespoon sugar
- 4 tablespoons vinegar
- ½ teaspoon paprika
- Black pepper to taste

Wash dandelion greens, roll in cloth, and pat dry. Put into a salad bowl, top with crumbled bacon and set in a warm place. Place butter and cream into a skillet and heat over low heat, melting the butter. Beat eggs, add salt, pepper, paprika, sugar, and vinegar, and mix with the slightly warm cream mixture. Cook over high heat until dressing is quite thick. Remove from heat and pour over the dandelion greens. Stir well and serve.

Tip: A crushed garlic clove rubbed on the inside of a salad bowl will heighten the taste of the salad's ingredients.

Wedge Salad with Warm Bacon Dressing

- 1 head iceberg lettuce
- 4 slices bacon
- 2 teaspoons brown sugar
- ¼ cup red wine vinegar
- Salt and freshly ground black pepper to taste
- 1 hard-boiled egg, finely chopped

Remove the core from the lettuce and cut into quarters. Arrange on serving plates and set aside. In a skillet, fry bacon pieces until crispy and place on paper towel-lined plate until cool enough to crumble. In the skillet in which the bacon was fried, add brown sugar and vinegar. Whisk together until combined. Cook over low heat until sugar is completely dissolved. Stir in the egg and bacon and season with salt and pepper to taste. Pour over the top of the iceberg wedges and serve immediately.

Creamy Waldorf Salad

- 2 3-ounce packages lemon-flavored gelatin
- 2 cups boiling water
- 1 cup cold water
- 1 3½-ounce package instant vanilla pudding mix
- 2 cups milk
- 1 cup diced apples
- ½ cup chopped celery
- ½ cup chopped nuts

Prepare lemon-flavored gelatin using the boiling water and the cold water. Set aside until partly set. Prepare pudding mix using the milk. Cool. Mix gelatin and pudding together. Add apples, celery, and nuts. Chill well before serving.

Household Hint

When cracking nuts, don't throw away the shell fragments that still have some nut meat left in them. Save them in a separate bowl and throw them out for the birds. With their small beaks, the birds will be able to pick out the hard-to-get pieces of nut.

Cream Cheese Salad

- 1 3-ounce package lime gelatin
- 2 cups boiling water
- 2 cups pineapple, drained
- 1 tablespoon unflavored gelatin
- ½ cup cold water
- 1 cup pineapple juice
- 6 ounces cream cheese
- 1 cup whipped cream
- 1 3-ounce package red gelatin
- 1¾ cups boiling water
- Whipped cream and mayonnaise to decorate
- Grated coconut, nuts, grated cheese *(optional)*

Dissolve the lime gelatin in 2 cups boiling water. Cool until syrupy. Add the pineapple. Pour into 2-quart mold. Set in refrigerator until firm. Dissolve unflavored gelatin in cold water. Heat pineapple juice. Add the gelatin and stir until dissolved. Remove from heat and cool. Mash up cream cheese and blend into the juice with beater. Stir in 1 cup whipped cream. Pour this on top of lime gelatin and let set until firm. Dissolve red gelatin in 1¾ cups boiling water. Cool well and pour over firm cream cheese layer. Set until all is firm. Serve on glass plate and decorate with whipped cream and mayonnaise. Sprinkle with grated coconut, nuts, or grated cheese if desired.

Fruited Cheese Salad

Serves 12
- 3 cups creamed-style cottage cheese
- 1 quart frozen whipped topping, thawed
- 1 3-ounce package each orange and pineapple gelatin
- 1 can pineapple tidbits, drained
- 1 small can mandarin oranges, drained

In mixer, blend cottage cheese and whipped topping. Stir in dry gelatin. Fold in pineapple tidbits and oranges and put in mold. Chill several hours.

Gelatin Salad

- 1 package lemon gelatin
- 1 teaspoon sugar
- 1 cup boiling water
- 1 cup milk
- 1 cup miniature marshmallows
- 2 tablespoons salad dressing
- 1 can fruit cocktail, well drained

Mix gelatin, sugar, and boiling water. Let stand until cooled but not set. Add milk, marshmallows, and salad dressing. Let stand until starting to set. Add fruit cocktail. Stir into gelatin mixture and let set.

Gracious words are a honeycomb, sweet to the soul and healing to the bones.

—Proverbs 16:24

Lime Gelatin Salad

- 1 package lime gelatin
- 2 cups boiling water
- 2 cups cold water
- 20 ounces crushed pineapple
- 2 cups miniature marshmallows
- 2–3 bananas, sliced
- 2 ounces slivered almonds *(optional)*

Dissolve gelatin in boiling water. Stir in cold water. Chill partially. Drain pineapple, reserving juice for another use if desired. Fold pineapple, sliced bananas, marshmallows, and almonds into gelatin. Pour into 7 x 12-inch pan. Chill until firm. Orange gelatin may be used as a substitute.

Orange Banana Salad

Dissolve the gelatin, sugar, and salt in the boiling water. Add orange juice, orange rind, and cold water. Measure 2 cups of mixture and chill to slightly thickened (set the remainder aside and chill until slightly thickened). Fold in orange sections and banana. Spoon into 6-cup mold and chill until almost firm. Whip the cream and fold into remaining gelatin. Spoon over gelatin in mold. Chill until firm.

Serves 8–10
- 1 6-ounce package banana-orange gelatin
- ⅓ cup sugar
- 2 cups boiling water
- ⅛ teaspoon salt
- ½ cup orange juice
- 1 teaspoon grated orange rind
- 1¼ cups cold water
- 1 cup diced orange sections
- 1 banana, sliced
- ½ cup cream

Tip: If you store ripe bananas in your refrigerator, they won't go soft so quickly. The cold temperature will darken the skins, but it won't affect the fruit.

Chicken Salad

- 2 cups cooked chicken, cubed
- 1 cup pineapple tidbits
- 1 cup orange sections
- 1 cup chopped celery
- 2 tablespoons orange juice
- 1 teaspoon marjoram
- ½ teaspoon salt
- 1 teaspoon vinegar
- ¼ cup mayonnaise

Mix all ingredients (except mayonnaise) and put in refrigerator for 1 hour before serving. Add mayonnaise, mix, and serve.

Cornbread Salad

- 1 large onion, diced
- 4 tomatoes, diced
- 1 green pepper, diced
- 4–5 stalks celery, diced
- 2 cups cauliflower, broken into small pieces
- 1 cup mayonnaise
- 1 tablespoon sugar
- 1 tablespoon sweet pickle relish
- 1 box Jiffy cornbread mix, baked the day before

Toss vegetables in a large bowl. Combine mayonnaise, sugar, and relish. Stir into vegetables. Cut cornbread into bite-size pieces and add to salad before serving.

A delicious treat!

Easy Taco Salad

- 1 pound ground beef
- 1 medium onion, chopped
- 1 package taco meat seasoning
- 1 15-ounce can red beans, rinsed
- 1 medium tomato, chopped
- 2 cups grated cheese
- Tortilla chips or corn chips, crushed
- French dressing (recipe on page 47)

Household Hint

For an inexpensive and very effective window cleaner, use slightly diluted white vinegar in a spray bottle. Wipe dry with a cloth. Vinegar will not leave streaks.

Brown the ground beef and onion. Drain. Add the taco seasoning. Mix together with the remaining ingredients in a large bowl and serve immediately.

Seven-Layer Lettuce Salad

- 1 head iceberg lettuce, cored and chopped
- 1 cup celery, chopped
- 1 cup red onion, chopped
- 1 10-ounce package frozen green peas, thawed, rinsed, and drained
- ½ pound cooked bacon, crumbled
- 3 hard-boiled eggs, chopped
- 1 pint mayonnaise
- 1 teaspoon sugar
- 1 cup grated cheddar cheese

Set aside some of the bacon to sprinkle on top. Layer first 6 ingredients, one at a time, in a large glass bowl so you can see each layer. Don't mix the ingredients. Mix the mayonnaise and sugar and spread evenly over the salad in the bowl. Add a layer of cheese, then a layer of bacon. Refrigerate until chilled.

Fruit Cream Dressing

- 3 tablespoons sugar
- 2 tablespoons flour
- 2 eggs
- 2 tablespoons vinegar
- 1 cup pear or pineapple juice
- 1 lemon rind and juice
- 1 cup cream or whipped topping substitute

Mix in order given (except cream) and cook in a double boiler over boiling water until thick. Before serving, add cream, whipped stiff, or whipped topping substitute.

✭ *This is a wonderful topping to embellish any gelatin salad, turning a simple salad into a delicious dessert!*

Mayonnaise

- 1 cup white sugar
- 2 eggs
- ¼ teaspoon salt, pepper
- 2 teaspoons dry mustard
- 2 teaspoons flour
- Scoop of butter the size of an egg
- ¾ cup vinegar
- ¾ cup water
- Cream

Photo courtesy of The Gray Boxwood, www.thegrayboxwood.com

Mix all together (except cream) and cook over low heat until thickened. When ready to use, mix equal parts of cream with mayonnaise.

Mustard

- 1 egg, beaten
- ¼ cup sugar
- 1 teaspoon cornstarch
- 4 teaspoons dry mustard
- 1 cup vinegar
- Salt to taste

Mix all together and boil until thickened.

The year is a never-ending adventure.

Hot Mustard

- 1 cup flour
- ¾ cup brown sugar
- ¾ teaspoon salt
- 5 tablespoons dry mustard
- 5 tablespoons prepared mustard
- 1 cup vinegar

Mix all together and store in jar.

Homemade French Dressing

- ½ cup sugar
- ¾ cup ketchup
- ¼ cup vinegar
- 1 cup salad oil
- ¼ cup water
- ½ teaspoon onion salt
- ½ teaspoon salt
- 1 teaspoon celery seed

Tip: When a jar of jam, mustard, or mayonnaise is almost empty, store the container on its side. This makes it easier to scrape out the last of the contents.

Put all ingredients in a quart jar. Shake very well or use a blender to mix all ingredients.

Simple Salad Dressing

- ½–1 cup sugar
- ½–1 cup vinegar (start with ½ cup and add more to taste if desired)
- 1 cup salad oil
- 1 10¾-ounce can tomato soup, undiluted
- 1 teaspoon dry mustard
- 1 teaspoon salt
- ½ teaspoon garlic powder
- 1 teaspoon celery seed
- 1 teaspoon pepper
- 1 clove garlic *(optional)*

Combine all ingredients in a quart jar. Shake well to combine. Store covered in the refrigerator.

Casseroles and Main Dishes

Chicken and Dressing Casserole

- 1 3–4 pound chicken
- 2 10¾-ounce cans cream of mushroom soup
- 1 medium onion, diced
- ¾ teaspoon poultry seasoning
- Salt and pepper to taste
- 20 slices dried bread, cubed
- Chicken broth
- 2 eggs, beaten

Cook chicken and remove meat from bones. Combine meat and mushroom soup. Set aside. Combine onion, seasoning, salt, pepper, and bread cubes with enough broth to moisten. Spread half the dressing over bottom of a 13 x 9-inch baking pan. Add chicken mixture. Add beaten eggs to remaining dressing. Spread over top of casserole. Bake at 350°F for 45 minutes.

Chicken Etti

- 1 8-ounce package spaghetti, broken into 2-inch pieces
- 3–4 cups cooked chicken, diced
- ¼ cup green pepper, diced
- 1 small onion, diced
- 1 can cream-based soup (chicken, mushroom, or celery)
- 1 cup chicken broth
- ¼ teaspoon salt
- ⅛ teaspoon celery salt
- ¼ teaspoon pepper
- ¾ pound grated Velveeta or cheddar cheese
- Bread crumbs, drizzled with melted butter *(optional)*

Cook the spaghetti with green pepper and onion until tender (about 12 minutes). Add the remaining ingredients, except the bread crumbs, and pour into a 1-quart casserole dish. Top with bread crumbs. Bake at 350°F for 25 minutes or until heated through.

Household Hint

To clean a tea kettle, use ¼ cup vinegar and 3 teaspoons salt, and boil for 15 minutes. This will save you from a lot of scrubbing!

Chicken Vegetable Casserole

Serves 8
- 2 cups cooked chicken, diced
- 2 10¾-ounce cans cream of mushroom soup
- 1 8-ounce can water chestnuts
- 1 small can mushrooms
- 1 16-ounce bag California mixed frozen vegetables
- 1 tablespoon finely chopped onion
- 4 ounces cheddar cheese

Mix together all ingredients in order given in a casserole dish. Bake covered at 350°F for 1 hour. Uncover and bake 15–20 minutes longer.

Chicken with Rice Casserole

- 1 3-pound chicken, cut up, or 3 pounds chicken legs or breasts, uncooked
- 1 cup uncooked rice
- 4 cups hot water
- 1 package onion soup mix
- 1 can mushroom soup
- 1 package chicken with rice soup mix or 1 tablespoon chicken broth concentrate
- Paprika (*optional*)

In the bottom of an oblong casserole, put rice, then chicken pieces. Dissolve soup mixes in water and pour over top, along with mushroom soup. Sprinkle paprika over top if desired. Bake at 350°F for 2 hours.

Ham and Noodle Bake

Serves 6

- 8 ounces noodles
- 3 cups cubed ham
- 1 medium onion, chopped
- 1 teaspoon salt
- Dash pepper
- 1 10¾-ounces can cream of chicken soup
- 1½ cups milk
- 1 cup sour cream
- 1 cup grated cheese

Cook noodles following package directions and drain. Brown ham and onion. Season with salt and pepper. Mix soup, milk, sour cream, and cheese together. Combine with noodles, ham, and onion in a casserole dish. Bake at 350°F for 30 minutes.

Ham, Potato, and Cheese Casserole

Serves 6 easily

- 1 medium onion, chopped
- 3 tablespoons chopped green pepper **(optional)**
- ¼ cup butter or margarine
- 2½ tablespoons flour
- 2 cups milk
- Salt and pepper to taste
- 3 cups cooked cubed potatoes
- 3 cups cooked cubed ham
- ¾ cup shredded cheese

Cook onion and green pepper in butter for 5 minutes. Add flour and stir. Add milk. Cook until thickened. Season with salt and pepper. Add potatoes and ham. Put in 2-quart casserole. Top with cheese. Bake at 350°F for 25–30 minutes.

Hamburger-Green Bean Casserole

- 1 pound ground beef
- 1 onion, chopped
- Salt and pepper to taste
- 1 14½-ounce can green beans, drained
- 2 8-ounce cans tomato sauce
  or 1 10¾-ounce can tomato soup
- Mashed potatoes
  (enough to cover casserole)

Brown beef and onion; drain. Season to taste. Spread over bottom of baking dish. Layer beans over meat mixture. Pour tomato sauce over beans. Spread mashed potatoes on top of everything. Bake at 350°F for 30–40 minutes.

Hamburger Tomato Casserole

Combine hamburger, tomatoes, and rice. Place in casserole and bake for 1½ hours at 350°F. About 30 minutes before serving, top with cheese slices and return to oven to finish cooking.

- 1 pound hamburger
- 1 quart canned tomatoes
- ¾ cup uncooked rice
- Salt and pepper to taste
- Cheese slices for top

 Great for a last-minute meal!!

Household Hint

To brighten dull silver, rub it with a piece of potato dipped in baking powder. Another way to brighten silver is to save the water left over from boiling potatoes. Soak your silver in this water.

Seven-Layer Dinner

- 1- to 2-inch layer of raw, sliced potatoes
- 1 layer raw, sliced onions
- 1 layer raw, sliced carrots
- ¼ cup quick-cooking rice
- 1 can peas, undrained
- 1 pound link-style pork sausage
- 1 10-ounce can tomato soup
- 1 soup can water
- Salt and pepper to taste

Arrange all ingredients in layers in deep, greased casserole. (Salt and pepper each layer.) Cover and bake 1 hour at 350°. Uncover and bake 15–30 minutes longer. Pork sausage can be substituted with 1½ pounds ground beef.

Tuna Noodle Casserole

- 1 onion, chopped
- 1 tablespoon butter
- 1 can cream of mushroom soup
- ½ cup milk
- 1 7-ounce can tuna, drained
- 1 cup cooked noodles
- ½ cup cooked peas, drained
- ½ cup shredded cheddar cheese

★ Family get-together favorite!!!

Cook onion in butter until browned. Combine with soup, milk, tuna, noodles, and peas. Pour into 1-quart casserole and top with cheese. Bake uncovered at 375°F for 25 minutes until hot and bubbling.

Baked Beef Stew

- 2 pounds beef stew meat, cut into 1-inch cubes
- 1 14½-ounce can diced tomatoes, undrained
- 3 tablespoons minute tapioca
- 1 can beef broth
- 2 teaspoons sugar
- 1½ teaspoons salt
- ¼ teaspoon pepper
- 4 carrots, cut into 1-inch pieces
- 2 stalks celery, cut into ¾-inch pieces
- 3 potatoes, peeled and cubed
- 1 medium onion, roughly chopped
- 1 slice bread, cubed

Brown beef cubes, drain, and set aside. Combine tomatoes, beef broth, tapioca, sugar, salt, and pepper. Stir in beef, vegetables, and bread cubes. Put into greased baking dish. Cover and bake at 375°F for 2 hours or until meat and vegetables are tender.

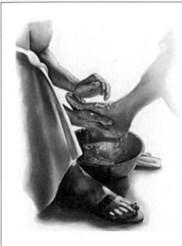

Foot Washing

While many of the outward observances of Amish and Mennonite faith remain in practice only among the conservative groups, foot washing is practiced in literal form almost universally from the most conservative Amish to the most modern, urban Mennonites. It is considered an act of humility and equality among church members. There are many stories of relationships restored as members release grievances against others through the foot-washing ceremony. It is based on the story found in **John 13:1-17**.

"When he had finished washing their feet, he put on his clothes and returned to his place. 'Do you understand what I have done for you?' he asked them. 'You call me 'Teacher' and 'Lord,' and rightly so, for that is what I am. Now that I, your Lord and Teacher, have washed your feet, you also should wash one another's feet.'"

Best-Ever Stew

- 2 pounds chuck or round steak, cubed
- 2 tablespoons oil
- 3 medium onions, cut in chunks
- 3 carrots, cut in chunks
- 4 stalks celery, cut in chunks
- 3–4 potatoes, cut in chunks
- 1 tablespoon tomato paste
- 3 tablespoons flour
- 2–3 cups beef broth
- Salt and pepper to taste

Brown meat in oil in heavy, ovenproof pan. Remove and set aside. Add vegetables to pan along with additional oil if needed. Brown slightly. Stir in tomato paste, flour, and broth. Season with salt and pepper. Return meat to pan and cook on top of stove until sauce is thickened. Bake at 325°F for 2 hours or until beef is tender. Store the remaining tomato paste by dropping tablespoons of the paste onto waxed paper. Freeze and store in small plastic bags. Use the next time you wish to make this stew.

Chuck Wagon Special

- 1 pound ground beef
- 1 package dry onion soup mix
- ½ cup water
- 1 cup ketchup
- 2 tablespoons prepared mustard
- 2 teaspoons vinegar
- 1 teaspoon Worcestershire sauce
- 1 teaspoon soy sauce
- 2 cans pork and beans
- 2–3 tablespoons brown sugar *(optional)*

Brown the ground beef, drain off excess grease, and add remaining ingredients. Put into a 9 x 13-inch casserole dish. Bake at 350°F for 30 minutes or until heated through. Can also cook in a slow cooker for 3–4 hours. May need to add additional water.

Household Hint

To remove grease from clothing, rub some shampoo on the spot, launder as usual, and the spot will be gone. This remedy even works on grease that has been set in clothing for a long time.

Haystacks

- 2 cups cooked rice
- 1 pound ground beef
- 1 small onion, chopped
- ¼ cup green pepper, chopped
- 1 package taco seasoning

Toppings:
- Chopped lettuce
- Chopped onion
- Chopped tomato
- Grated cheese or cheese sauce
- Crushed corn chips

Brown ground beef, onion, and green pepper. Drain. Add taco seasoning. Put toppings in separate bowls. Everyone builds their own haystack by starting with crushed corn chips on their plates, pouring the hamburger mixture over the cooked rice, and adding toppings as desired.

Household Hint

To keep your outdoor tools from being lost in the yard, paint the handles bright red or orange.

Impossible Cheeseburger Pie

Makes 6–8 servings
- 1 pound ground beef
- 1½ cups chopped onion
- ½ teaspoon salt
- ¼ teaspoon pepper
- 1½ cups milk
- ¾ cup baking mix
- 3 eggs
- 2 tomatoes, sliced
- 1 cup shredded cheddar cheese

Heat oven to 400°F. Grease a 1 ½-inch-deep 10-inch pie plate. Brown beef and onion. Drain. Stir in salt and pepper. Spread meat mixture in pie plate. Beat milk, baking mix, and eggs until smooth (15 seconds in blender on high or 1 minute with hand beater). Pour over meat mixture. Bake 25 minutes. Immediately top with tomatoes and sprinkle with cheese. Bake 5 minutes more.

Juicy Meat Loaf

- 1½ pounds ground beef
- ¼ pound ground pork
- ¼ cup finely cut onion
- 1 cup quick-cooking or regular rolled oats
- 2 teaspoons salt
- ¼ teaspoon pepper
- ½ teaspoon dry mustard or 2½ teaspoons prepared mustard
- ¼ cup ketchup
- 1 egg, beaten
- 1 cup water or milk
- Parsley sprigs

Mix all ingredients except parsley thoroughly. Pack into a 9 x 5-inch loaf pan. Bake at 375°F for 1–1½ hours. Slice and serve garnished with parsley sprigs.

 ## Household Hint

To remove paint or varnish from wood, use a mixture of two parts ammonia to one part turpentine.

Poor Boy Beef Fillets

- 1½ pounds ground beef
- 1 cup applesauce, or 2 raw apples peeled and ground
- 1 cup shredded carrots
- ½ cup quick oatmeal
- 2 eggs
- 1 small onion
- Salt, pepper, and garlic to taste
- Bacon

Combine all ingredients except bacon. Shape into fillets and wrap each with a strip of bacon around edge and secure with toothpicks. Put in greased pan and bake at 350°F for 45 to 50 minutes.

Poor Man's Steak

- 3 pounds ground beef
- 1 cup cracker crumbs
- 1 cup cold water
- Salt and pepper to taste
- Flour
- Oil
- 1 can mushroom soup

Mix ground beef, cracker crumbs, and cold water together in a large bowl. Press mixture into a cookie sheet and chill long enough to set. Cut in squares and roll in flour seasoned with salt and pepper. Fry on both sides in a small amount of oil until golden brown; don't overcook. Place in a baking dish. Pour can of undiluted mushroom soup over top. Bake at 325°F for 1½–2 hours.

✳ This recipe is always a surprise for guests. It tastes like a delicious cut of beef rather than just ground beef.

Porcupine Meatballs

- 1 pound hamburger
- 4 slices bread
- 1 egg, beaten
- 1 cup milk
- 1 onion
- ¼ cup uncooked rice
- 2 cups tomato juice

Crumble bread and soak in milk. Add beaten egg. Mix with other ingredients (except tomato juice). Shape into balls and place in casserole. Pour tomato juice over top and bake 1½ hours at 350°F.

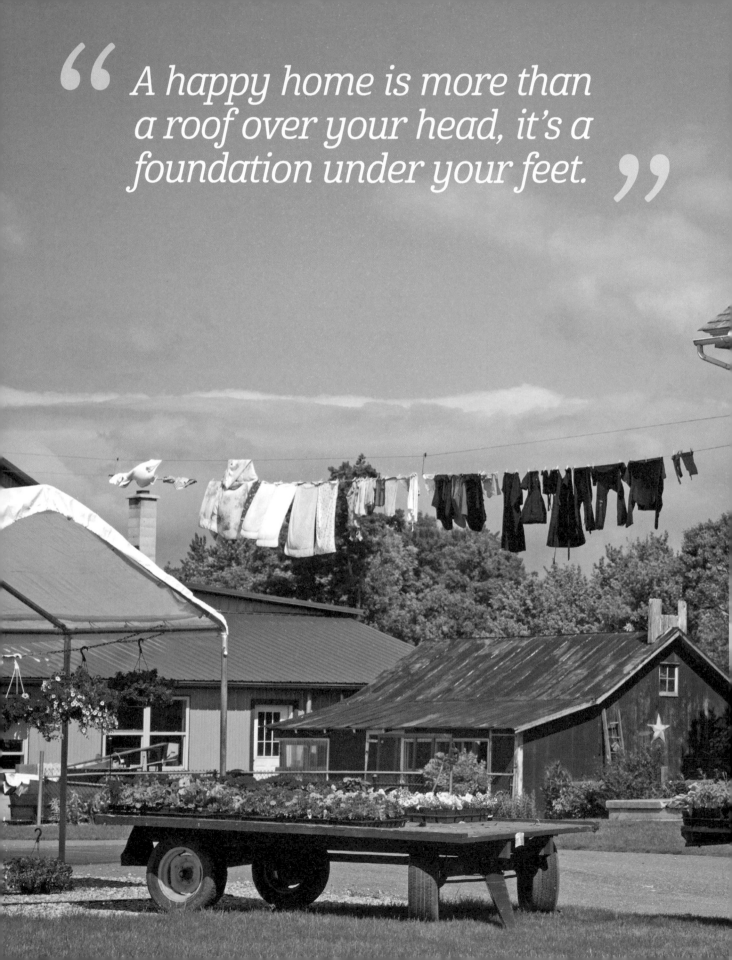

> "A happy home is more than a roof over your head, it's a foundation under your feet."

Round Steak for Sunday Dinner

- Round steak
- Flour
- Salt and pepper
- Oil
- Water

Purchase a round steak and have butcher tenderize it, or purchase the more expensive minute steak. Cut into serving pieces, dredge both sides with flour seasoned with salt and pepper. Brown the pieces in a small amount of oil. This can be done in a frying pan on top of stove or in flat baking pans in the oven at 350°F.

When browned on both sides, place meat in layers in a small roasting pan. Add a small amount of water. Bake at 350°F for the first 30 minutes. Check the amount of water and add more if necessary. Cover meat with foil then cover with the lid. Turn oven to 125°F. Bake for 2 hours or so until steak is fork tender.

Saucy Barbecued Meatballs

- 3 pounds ground beef
- 2 cups oatmeal
- 2 cups milk
- 2 eggs, beaten
- 1 onion, chopped
- 2 teaspoons salt
- ½ teaspoon pepper
- 2 teaspoons chili powder

Sauce:
- 2 cups ketchup
- 2 cups water
- 3 cups brown sugar
- 4 tablespoons liquid smoke
- 1 teaspoon garlic powder

Mix all ingredients together and form 1-inch meatballs. Place in a baking dish. Mix sauce ingredients and pour over top. Bake at 350°F for 1 hour.

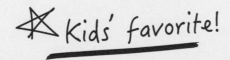

Kids' favorite!

Sloppy Joes

- 1 pound ground beef
- ¼ cup chopped onion
- 1 tablespoon Worcestershire sauce
- 2 tablespoons brown sugar
- 1 tablespoon vinegar
- 1 teaspoon prepared mustard
- ½ cup ketchup
- 1 teaspoon salt
- 6–8 hamburger buns
  (or other rolls of choice)

Sauté beef in skillet and drain off fat. Add next 7 ingredients in list and simmer 15–30 minutes. Serve on hamburger buns.

Swiss Steak

Serves 8

- 3 tablespoons fat
- 2 pounds round steak, 1-inch thick
- ½ cup flour
- 1½ teaspoons salt
- ¼ teaspoon pepper
- 1 10¾-ounce can cream of mushroom soup
- 1 soup can water

Melt fat in skillet. Cut steak into small pieces and roll/dredge in a mixture of the flour, salt, and pepper. Brown steak on both sides. Transfer meat to a baking dish or roaster. Combine mushroom soup and water. Pour over steak. Cover and bake at 350°F for 1½ hours.

 Tip: Dropping a few tomatoes in the pot will help tenderize a roast. Acid from the tomatoes helps break down the roast's stringy fibers.

Barbecued Spareribs

Serves 5

- 3 pounds spareribs
- 1 medium onion, chopped
- 1 tablespoon butter
- 1 tablespoon vinegar
- 1 tablespoon sugar
- 2 teaspoons salt
- 3 tablespoons lemon juice
- ½ tablespoon prepared mustard
- ½ cup water
- ½ cup chopped celery
- Dash of pepper
- 1– 2 tablespoons Worcestershire sauce **(optional)**

Wipe ribs with damp cloth and cut into serving size pieces. Place in a shallow baking pan and bake uncovered at 350°F for 30 minutes. Meanwhile, lightly brown onion in butter, then add remaining ingredients. Mix well and simmer 5 minutes. Pour over the spareribs and continue baking for 1 hour longer, basting ribs from time to time with the sauce in the bottom of the pan.

Tip: To clean your barbecue or oven racks, place them on the grass overnight or on a rainy day. The cleanup job is easier!

Smoky Country-Style Ribs

Serves 4–6

- 4 pounds country-style ribs
- Garlic salt to taste
- Fresh ground pepper to taste
- 1¼ cup ketchup
- ¾ cup firmly packed brown sugar
- ½ cup chili sauce
- 2 tablespoons vinegar
- 2 tablespoons liquid smoke seasoning
- 1 tablespoon lemon juice

Sprinkle ribs with garlic salt and pepper. Combine remaining ingredients in medium saucepan. Cook over medium heat for about 10 minutes, stirring occasionally. Keep warm. Place ribs, rib bones down, on a rack in a shallow roasting pan. Baste with sauce. Bake at 325°F for 1½– 2 hours, turning and basting with sauce every 30 minutes. Cut into serving portions. Heat remaining sauce and serve with ribs.

Sweet and Sour Pig Tails or Spareribs

- Pig tails or spareribs

Sauce:
- ¼ cup brown sugar
- 3 tablespoons cornstarch
- ¼ teaspoon dry mustard
- ⅛ teaspoon ginger
- 1 teaspoon salt
- ¾ teaspoon chili powder
- 1 clove garlic
- 5 tablespoons vinegar
- 1 cup tomato juice
- 1 cup water
- 1 teaspoon soy sauce
- Mushrooms, green pepper, red pepper (*optional*)

Mix all sauce ingredients and cook until thickened, stirring frequently. Pour over pig tails or ribs in roasting pan. Bake in oven 1 hour. Add mushrooms, green pepper, and red pepper if desired and bake 1 more hour.

 Gameday Snack!!

Ham Loaf

Grind together the ham, pork, and beef (or have butcher grind them together). Add bread crumbs, eggs, and tomato juice to meat. Mix well. Form into loaves. Combine sauce ingredients and pour over loaves. Bake at 350°F for 1¼ hours. Baste with sauce mixture during baking.

- 3 pounds smoked ham
- 1 pound fresh pork
- 1 pound beef
- 2 cups bread crumbs
- 4 eggs, beaten
- 1 cup tomato juice

Sauce:
- ½ cup brown sugar
- ¼ cup vinegar
- ½ cup pineapple juice

Pork and Beans

- 5 pounds white beans, soaked overnight
- ½ teaspoon nutmeg
- ½ teaspoon pepper
- ½ teaspoon mustard
- 4 tablespoons molasses
- 2 tablespoons salt
- 2 pounds diced bacon or 1 ham bone
- Ketchup to taste

Combine ingredients, except ketchup, and boil until beans are tender. Add ketchup to suit taste and simmer 10–15 minutes. If canning, steam pints 15 minutes and quarts 30 minutes. Instead of bacon, you can use 1 ham bone, which can be removed when beans are cooked.

 Tip: Bacon will curl less during frying if it has first been soaked in cold water.

Pork Chops

Serves 6

- 6 lean pork chops cut ¾-inch thick
- 1 tablespoon oil
- 4 cups sliced apples
- ¼ cup raisins
- ¼ teaspoon cinnamon
- 1 teaspoon grated lemon peel **(optional)**
- ¼ cup brown sugar
- ¼ cup water

Brown chops in oil in electric fry pan at 380°F. Cover and cook at 200°F until tender (about 30 minutes). Pour off fat. Add apples, raisins, cinnamon, lemon peel, brown sugar, and water. Cover and cook until apples are tender (15–20 minutes). Serve on warmed platter.

Tip: A mixture of olive oil and vinegar will tenderize meat. Rub the mixture on the meat and let it stand several hours before cooking.

Simple Pork and Sauerkraut

Serves 8–10

- 1 10- to 15-pound pork shoulder
- 4 pounds sauerkraut (canned or bagged), with juice
- Salt and pepper to taste

Preheat oven to 350°F. Rinse pork and place in large roasting pan. Sprinkle with salt and pepper to taste. Cover with ⅓ of the sauerkraut. Cover roasting pan and put in oven for 1 ½ hours. Remove from oven and add another ⅓ of sauerkraut. Cover and put back in oven for another hour. Remove from oven and add the remaining sauerkraut. Cover and put back in oven for another hour. Remove from oven and enjoy.

Pork and Sauerkraut

- 2 tablespoons oil
- 4 ¾-inch-thick pork chops
- 2 cloves garlic, minced
- 1 onion, thinly sliced
- 16 ounces sauerkraut
- 1 teaspoon caraway seed
- 2 tablespoons apple juice
- Salt and pepper to taste

Heat oil in a large skillet over medium heat. Brown pork chops on all sides and remove from pan. Add garlic, onion, sauerkraut, caraway seed, apple juice, and salt and pepper to the hot skillet. Sauté for 3 to 4 minutes. Lay browned chops on top of sauerkraut mixture, cover, reduce heat to low, and cook for 20 minutes, stirring occasionally.

Chicken Pot Pie

- 1 chicken (boiling fowl preferred)
- 4 potatoes, quartered
- Salt and pepper to taste
- Chicken broth mix to taste
- Parsley to taste

Dough:
- 1½ cups flour
- ½ teaspoon salt
- 2 eggs
- 3 tablespoons cream

To prepare chicken, cut into pieces. Add water to cover and cook until meat is done. Remove meat. Season broth to taste and add water to make at least 4 cups. You may need some additional commercial chicken broth mix, salt, pepper, and parsley to season it. Add potatoes.

To prepare dough, mix flour and salt and create a well in the center. Pour in egg and cream, and stir into a soft dough. Roll thin and cut into 2- to 3-inch squares or triangles. Drop carefully on surface of boiling broth. Each piece should remain flat. Cook 30 minutes in tightly covered pot. Serve in large tureen that has the warm chicken and broth in the bottom.

Tip: For guaranteed tenderness, marinate chicken breasts in buttermilk, cream, or ordinary milk for three hours in the refrigerator before baking.

Cranberry Chicken

- 8 pieces of chicken
- 1 cup flour, seasoned with salt, pepper, and cayenne pepper to taste
- 1 16-ounce can whole cranberries
- 1 16-ounce can cranberry sauce
- 1 cup onion, chopped
- ¾ cup orange juice
- ¼ teaspoon ground ginger
- ¼ teaspoon cinnamon

Combine and heat cranberries, cranberry sauce, onion, orange juice, and spices in a saucepan or microwave oven. Bring to a boil and set aside. Dredge chicken pieces with the seasoned flour and lightly brown on all sides in a frying pan; do not overcook. Transfer to a greased baking dish, pour cranberry mixture over chicken, and bake at 350°F for 30–45 minutes or until tender.

Easy Garden Vegetable Pie

- 2 cups sliced fresh broccoli or cauliflower
- ½ cup chopped onion
- ½ cup chopped green pepper
- 1 cup shredded cheddar cheese
- 1½ cups milk
- 3 eggs
- ¾ cup baking mix
- 1 teaspoon salt
- ¼ teaspoon pepper

Heat oven to 400°F. Lightly grease a 1½-inch-deep 10-inch pie pan. Heat 1 inch salted water to a boil. Add broccoli. Cover and heat to boiling. Cook until almost tender (about 5 minutes). Drain thoroughly. Mix broccoli, onion, green pepper, and cheese in pie pan. Place milk, eggs, baking mix, and salt and pepper in blender. Blend for 15 seconds and pour over vegetables.

Bake 35–40 minutes or until golden brown. Test by inserting a knife in center of pie. It's done when the knife comes out clean. Let stand for a few minutes before cutting. One 10-ounce package of frozen, chopped broccoli or cauliflower, thawed and drained, can be substituted for the fresh vegetables.

Verenike

Prepare a soft dough from the ingredients listed. Roll out thin and cut in circles using a tin can 4 inches in diameter. Combine ingredients for cottage cheese filling. Place a spoonful of filling on each circle. Fold and seal edges well. Cook in boiling water until they float, or deep fry in fat until golden brown. Top with cream gravy.

- 21 cups flour
- 12 eggs
- 2 tablespoons salt
- 2 cups cream
- 4 cups milk

Filling:
- 8 cups well-drained cottage cheese
- 2 eggs
- 2 teaspoons salt
- ½ teaspoon pepper

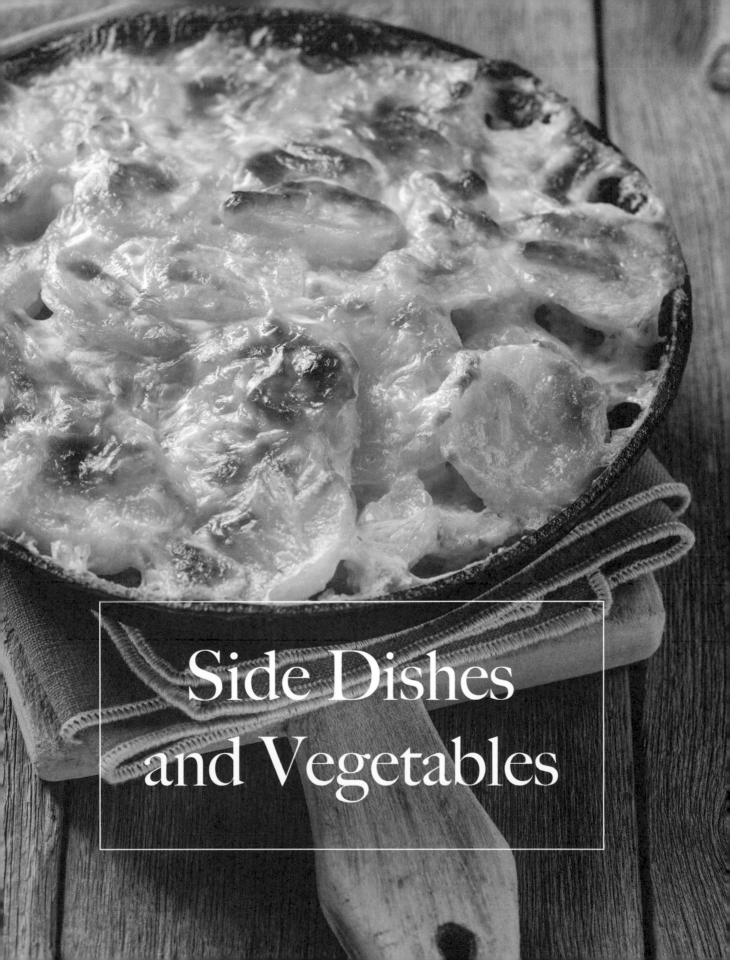

Side Dishes and Vegetables

Baked Corn

- 2 cups corn
- 2 tablespoons butter
- 1 tablespoon sugar
- 1 teaspoon salt
- ⅛ teaspoon pepper
- 2 eggs
- 1 cup milk
- 1½ tablespoons flour
- ½ cup bread crumbs *(optional)*

Combine all ingredients (except bread crumbs) and mix in a blender or with a mixer. Put in a 2-quart greased casserole dish. Bake at 350°F for 45 minutes or until center is done. Sprinkle bread crumbs over the top if desired.

Broccoli-Corn Bake

- 1 10-ounce package chopped broccoli, cooked and drained
- ½ cup saltine cracker crumbs
- ½ teaspoon salt
- 5 tablespoons melted butter, divided
- 1 can cream-style corn
- 1 egg, beaten
- ¼ cup chopped onion
- Dash pepper
- 1 cup bread cubes, finely cut

Combine 3 tablespoons butter with broccoli, corn, egg, cracker crumbs, onion, and seasonings. Pour into buttered 1½-quart casserole dish. Combine bread cubes and remaining 2 tablespoons butter and sprinkle over top of vegetables. Bake uncovered at 350°F for 35–40 minutes.

 Pride in your work puts joy in your day.

Corn Casserole

- 1 can cream-style corn
- 1 can whole-kernel corn
- ½ cup (1 stick) margarine, melted
- 1 cup sour cream
- 1 box cornbread muffin mix
- 2 eggs, beaten

Thoroughly mix all ingredients. Pour into a 9 x 13-inch baking pan. Bake at 350°F for 30 minutes.

Photo courtesy of The Gray Boxwood, www.thegrayboxwood.com

Creamed Dried Corn

To dry corn, cut kernels off corncobs. Spread thinly on cookie sheets and dry in 250°F oven. Stir often. Leave oven door open slightly for steam to escape. Remove when kernels are hard and brown in color. Store in a tight container for as long as you wish. When ready to serve, combine the dried corn with the boiling water and salt. Boil until corn is soft, adding water as necessary. Make a paste of flour and water. Add and boil until thick. Add the cream.

Serves 4
- 2 cups dried corn
- 3 cups boiling water
- Salt to taste
- Flour
- ½ cup cream

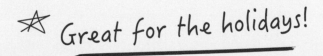

★ Great for the holidays!

Scalloped Corn

- 2 cups corn
- 1 cup milk
- ⅔ cup cracker crumbs
- 1 tablespoon sugar
- 1 teaspoon onion
- Salt to taste
- ⅛ teaspoon pepper
- 2 eggs
- ½ cup butter, melted

Beat eggs, add milk, sugar, and cracker crumbs. Add corn, onion, and seasoning to butter. Pour egg mixture into corn and butter and mix well. Pour into greased casserole dish. Bake at 350°F for 40 minutes.

Amish Potatoes

- 3 tablespoons butter
- 8 potatoes, cooked and sliced
- 1½ cups half-and-half
- Salt and pepper to taste

Melt butter in skillet. Add sliced potatoes and brown slightly. Add half-and-half and simmer until potatoes absorb the cream. Add salt and pepper to taste. You can also cook the potatoes and half-and-half in a slow cooker.

Tip: When cooking potatoes or rice, add a pinch of rosemary to the water instead of salt; it adds a special flavor.

Apricot Sweet Potatoes

Serves 8
- 1 cup brown sugar
- 1½ tablespoons cornstarch
- 1 teaspoon grated orange peel
- ¼ teaspoon salt
- ⅛ teaspoon cinnamon
- 1 5½-ounce can apricot nectar
- ⅓ cup water
- 2 tablespoons butter
- 1 18-ounce can sweet potatoes, drained
- 12 frozen (or 1 can) apricots
- ½ cup pecans *(optional)*

Mix sugar, cornstarch, orange peel, salt, and cinnamon in a heavy 1-quart saucepan. Stir in apricot nectar and water. Stir on high heat until mixture comes to a full rolling boil. Stir in butter. Layer sweet potatoes and apricots in a greased casserole. Pour hot sauce over top. Sprinkle with pecans if desired. Bake uncovered at 375°F for 25 minutes or until hot and bubbly.

Household Hint:

Pureed leftover vegetables lend additional flavor to soup stocks. If soup isn't on the menu, freeze the puree in ice cube trays and use the vegetable "cubes" later as needed.

Cheesy Scalloped Potatoes

- 6 potatoes
- ½ cup butter
- ½ cup chopped onion
- ½ teaspoon parsley flakes
- 1 teaspoon mustard
- 1 teaspoon salt
- ¼ teaspoon pepper
- ¼ cup milk
- ½ pound Velveeta cheese

Boil potatoes in skins. Peel when cooled and dice coarsely. Melt cheese in milk and add other ingredients. Stir in potatoes. Bake at 325°F for 45 minutes or until bubbly.

Creamed Potatoes

- Potatoes
- Salt
- Water
- Heavy cream
- Sweet marjoram or parsley

Slice potatoes thinly. Add salt and some water. Cook until potatoes are tender. Add heavy cream and sprinkle with sweet marjoram or parsley.

A friend is like a rainbow—always there for you after a storm.

—**Suzanne Woods Fisher**

Make-Ahead Mashed Potatoes for a Crowd

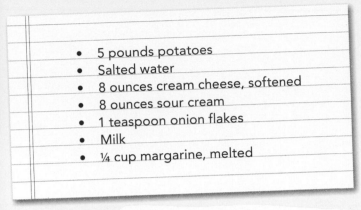

- 5 pounds potatoes
- Salted water
- 8 ounces cream cheese, softened
- 8 ounces sour cream
- 1 teaspoon onion flakes
- Milk
- ¼ cup margarine, melted

Peel potatoes and boil in salted water. Drain. Add cream cheese, sour cream, and onion flakes. Mash or whip, adding enough milk for the desired consistency. Spread in a buttered 9 x 13-inch pan. Drizzle melted margarine over top when ready to use. Bake at 350°F for 1 hour.

Tip: Mashed potatoes can always round out a good dinner, but having to mash them right before you eat adds just one more thing to do when you are busy preparing a big meal. This dish can be prepared the day before. Just cover and refrigerate for 24 hours, giving you a head start on your meal.

Barbecued Green Beans

Brown bacon and onion in small skillet. Combine with beans in a casserole dish. Mix remaining ingredients in pot and simmer 2 minutes. Pour over bean mixture. Bake at 350°F for 20–30 minutes.

- 2 bacon strips, diced
- 2 tablespoons chopped onion
- 1 14½-ounce can green beans, drained
- ¼ cup ketchup
- 2 tablespoons brown sugar
- 1½ teaspoons Worcestershire sauce

Living the Simple Life

Here are some common Amish sayings and their English meanings.

"She is wonderful poor," means, "She is extremely poor."

"Don't splutter so," means, "Don't talk so fast."

"You liked it still," means, "You used to like it."

Source—Mindy Starns Clark

"We live simply so that others may simply live."

Hearty Baked Beans

- 1 2½-pound can lima beans
- 1 medium onion, chopped
- ½ medium green pepper, chopped
- ½ cup brown sugar
- About ⅓ bottle ketchup
- 8 bacon strips

Place beans, onion, and green pepper in a casserole dish. Mix well. Blend brown sugar and ketchup. Stir into bean mixture. Fry bacon. Break into pieces and stir into beans. Bake at 300°F for 1½–2 hours.

Sweet and Sour Beans

- 8 bacon slices
- 1–2 small onions
- ¾ cup brown sugar
- 1 teaspoon salt
- ½ teaspoon dry mustard
- ½ teaspoon garlic salt
- ½ teaspoon vinegar
- 5 pints beans, drained

Chop bacon and onion, fry lightly; drain off grease. Add remaining ingredients (except beans). Cook 1 minute. Add beans, using at least 3–4 kinds. Bake at 350°F for 1 hour. Can also be cooked in a slow cooker for 3–4 hours. Add a little water if using the slow cooker.

Tip: Try using green, yellow, lima, kidney, or red beans, or canned pork and beans.

Glazed Carrots

- 1 pound carrots, scraped and sliced on the diagonal
- ¼ cup butter
- ½ cup brown sugar

Cook carrots in a small amount of water until tender-crisp. Drain. Melt butter in a separate pot. Stir in sugar until well blended. Add carrots. Cook, stirring frequently, until syrup comes to a boil (about 10 minutes) and carrots are evenly coated/glazed. Carrots may also be put in a baking dish and baked at 300°F for 30–45 minutes. Stir every 10 minutes to coat evenly.

Carrot Casserole

Parboil the carrots for a few minutes. Sauté the onion in the butter. Drain carrots, put in baking dish, and pour onion and butter mixture over top. In a saucepan or microwave oven, melt the Velveeta cheese and evaporated milk together. Pour over carrot mixture and bake covered at 350°F for 20 minutes. Top with crushed corn flakes and bake uncovered 10 minutes longer. Serve immediately.

- 4 cups carrots, sliced
- 1 medium onion, chopped
- ½ cup butter
- ¾ pound Velveeta cheese
- ⅓ cup evaporated milk
- Crushed corn flakes (enough to cover casserole)

Tip: If you're simmering vegetables and you need to add more water, use hot water, not cold. Adding cold water may toughen the vegetable fibers.

Zucchini Casserole

- 3 cups grated zucchini
- ½ cup onion
- 1 cup all-purpose baking mix
- 4 eggs, slightly beaten
- ½ cup Parmesan cheese
- 1 cup grated Swiss cheese
- 1 tablespoon dried parsley
- ½ teaspoon salt
- ½ teaspoon pepper
- ½ cup oil

Mix all ingredients together and put in 7 x 12-inch baking pan. Bake at 350°F for 30–35 minutes or until a knife comes out clean when inserted in the center.

Hot Pineapple Side Dish

- 1 20-ounce can pineapple chunks or tidbits, undrained
- ½ cup sugar
- 3 tablespoons flour
- ½ cup butter, melted
- 1½ cups shredded cheddar cheese, divided
- 2 cups crushed Ritz crackers

Drain pineapple juice and reserve ¼ cup. Combine sugar, flour, and 1 cup cheese. Cover the bottom of a greased baking dish with the pineapple. Spoon sugar, flour, and cheese mixture over pineapple. Spread crushed Ritz crackers over the mixture and drizzle melted butter and ¼ cup reserved juice over all. Bake uncovered at 350°F for 30 to 35 minutes. Sprinkle remaining ½ cup of cheese on top.

Tip: This is a wonderful side dish to add to any meal. Your guests will love it, but may have a hard time figuring out exactly what it is since hot pineapple is not a typical side dish. Give it a try!

Barbecued Kraut

- 4 bacon strips, diced
- ½ onion, sliced
- ½ cup brown sugar
- 1 8-ounce can tomato sauce
- Dash each of A1 steak sauce, Worcestershire sauce, and barbecue sauce
- 2 pounds sauerkraut, drained and rinsed

Brown diced bacon and drain grease. Combine bacon with remaining ingredients in mixing bowl. Mix well. Transfer to slow cooker and simmer on high setting for 3 hours.

Rice Pilaf

- 1 cup rice
- 1 cup diced celery
- ¾ cup diced onion
- 3 tablespoons butter
- ½ teaspoon thyme
- ¼ teaspoon rubbed sage
- ¼ teaspoon black pepper
- 2½ cups water
- 1 package dry chicken noodle soup mix

Sauté the rice, celery, and onion in the butter until the rice begins to turn a little brown. Add remaining ingredients and bring to a boil. Reduce heat, cover, and simmer for 15 minutes. Remove from heat and let stand 10 minutes before removing lid.

Tip: Buying a boxed rice pilaf can be costly, especially if you are feeding a crowd. This recipe is simple, quick, and delicious; you will never buy a box of rice pilaf again once you try it.

Easy Dressing for Turkey

- 1 loaf bread, cubed
- 2 chopped onions
- 1 cup water
- ½ cup butter
- Salt, pepper, poultry seasoning, and parsley to taste

For each loaf of bread, boil 2 onions in 1 cup water for 5 minutes. Add ¼ pound (or less) butter. When butter is melted, pour liquid over chopped bread. Season to taste with salt, pepper, poultry seasoning, and parsley. A large turkey will take 2 loaves of bread.

Bread Stuffing

Serves 8–10
- ¼ teaspoon saffron thread, crumbled
- 1 cup milk
- ½ medium onion, finely chopped
- 2 stalks celery and leaves, finely chopped
- 1 tablespoon butter
- 1 egg, beaten
- 6 cups white bread, cut in cubes
- 2 tablespoons parsley, finely chopped
- ¼ teaspoon salt
- Fresh ground pepper to taste

Sauté the chopped onion and celery in melted butter over low heat until soft. Add all the milk and saffron to the beaten egg and pour it over the bread. When the celery and onion are soft, mix all ingredients together. Bake in an uncovered buttered casserole at 350°F for about 30 minutes, until it forms a crust.

Brown Butter Noodles

Serves 4–6
- 1 12-ounce package egg noodles
- ½ cup butter

Prepare noodles as directed on the package. In a saucepan, melt butter over medium heat, stirring until it begins to brown. Once butter is golden brown, remove from heat and pour over noodles immediately.

Tip: For an added crunch, sauté breadcrumbs in butter in a heavy saucepan until golden brown and crispy. Sprinkle on top of noodles just before serving. So delicious—it's a dish everyone will love!

Homemade Noodles

- 3 egg yolks
- 1 whole egg
- 3 tablespoons cold water
- 1 teaspoon salt
- 2 cups flour
- 3 tablespoons oil (*optional*)

Beat eggs until light. Beat in water, oil (optional), and salt. Work in flour. Divide dough into 3 parts. Roll each part as thin as possible in 3 circles. Place each circle between 2 towels until dough is partially dry. When partially dry, roll each circle as you would a jelly roll. Cut with a sharp knife into desired width. Spread out and let dry well before using or storing. These keep well in the freezer.

Traditional Noodles

- 6 eggs
- 4 tablespoons cold water
- ½ teaspoon salt
- 4 cups all-purpose flour

Mix the eggs, cold water, and salt well. Add the flour and knead about 100 times. Roll thin and cut in strips of width desired. Allow to dry thoroughly and store in jars or plastic containers.

Living the Simple Life

Here are some common Amish sayings and their English meanings.

"The cookies are all, but the milk is yet," means, "The cookies are all gone, but some milk is left."

"I must change around," means, "I need to change my clothes"

"Will it give rain?" means, "Will it make rain?"

Source—Mindy Starns Clark

Breads and
Breakfast Foods

Amish Friendship Bread Starter

- Flour
- Sugar
- Yeast
- Water
- Milk

This starter recipe and the bread recipe on the following page are known as "friendship bread" because they are meant to be shared! The entire starter recipe takes 10 days to make, and when you are finished, you will have 4–7 portions, 1 to keep for yourself, and the rest to present to your friends. And be sure to give them a sample of the finished bread, too! Then your friends can make their own bread and continue the sharing.

Day 1: In a large bowl, mix ¼ cup water and 1 (¼ oz) package active dry yeast. Add 1 cup flour, 1 cup sugar, and 1 cup milk, and mix thoroughly. Cover bowl with plastic wrap and leave in a warm, draft-free place for 24 hours.

Days 2, 3, and 4: Gently stir the starter about 10 times each day.

Day 5: Add 1 cup flour, 1 cup sugar, and 1 cup milk to the starter. Stir thoroughly and wrap with plastic wrap again. Return to a warm, draft-free place.

Days 6, 7, 8, and 9: Gently stir the starter about 10 times each day.

Day 10: Add 1 cup flour, 1 cup sugar, and 1 cup milk to the starter. The starter should be creamy in consistency and pourable, like a rather thick batter. Measure out equal portions of 1 cup each into 4 1-gallon zipper bags. You will usually end up with 4–7 portions depending on how active your starter has been. Keep one of the bags for yourself (or leave it in the mixing bowl if you plan to bake right away), and give the other bags to friends, along with the recipe. Starter portions can also be kept in the freezer until needed for next time.

If you don't pass this recipe on to a friend on Day 1 or Day 10, make sure to tell them which day it is when you present it to them.

"You can tell how big a person is by what it takes to discourage him."

Amish Friendship Bread

Makes 2 loaves

- ⅔ cup oil
- 3 eggs
- ½ teaspoon salt
- 1 teaspoon vanilla
- 1 teaspoon cinnamon
- 1 cup sugar
- 2 cups flour
- 1¼ teaspoons baking powder
- ½ teaspoon baking soda
- ½ cup fruit or nuts *(optional)*

In a large bowl, combine all ingredients with 1 cup of Amish Friendship Bread Starter (see previous page). Using a fork, beat by hand until well blended. Grease two loaf pans with butter and sprinkle with sugar instead of flour. Bake at 325°F for 45 minutes to 1 hour. Cool 10 minutes, remove from pans.

Tip: To prevent pastry dough from clinging to your rolling pin, chill the pin in the freezer before flouring.

Baking Powder Biscuits

- 1 cup flour
- 4 teaspoons baking powder
- ½ teaspoon salt
- 2 tablespoons sugar
- ½ heaping cup shortening
- 1 egg unbeaten
- ⅔ cup milk

Combine dry ingredients. Blend in shortening with pastry cutter until a cornmeal consistency. Add milk slowly as you stir. Add egg and stir until a stiff dough. Knead on a lightly floured surface 5 times. Do not over-knead. Roll out dough and cut. Bake at 400–450°F for 10 to 15 minutes.

 Tip: The name may not sound exciting, but these biscuits are so light and delectable your family will be asking for more. They are especially delicious piping hot from the oven smothered with butter and honey.

Christmas Bread

- ½ cup butter
- 1 cup sugar
- 2 eggs
- 1 teaspoon vanilla
- 1 teaspoon baking soda
- ½ teaspoon salt
- 2 cups flour
- 1 cup mashed ripe bananas
- 1 cup mandarin oranges, drained
- 1 cup flaked coconut
- 1 cup chocolate chips
- ⅔ cup sliced almonds, divided
- ½ cup chopped maraschino cherries
- ½ cup chopped dates

Beat butter and sugar until creamy. Add eggs and vanilla; beat well. Combine flour, salt, and baking soda; add to butter mixture alternately with the mashed bananas. Stir in remaining ingredients using only half the almonds. Spoon into 2 loaf pans that have been well greased. Sprinkle remaining almonds on top. Bake at 350°F for 50–55 minutes. Cool in pan for 10 minutes before removing.

Tip: The best way to use up overripe bananas is to use them for breads or cakes.

Dutch Honey Bread

- 1 cup honey
- 1 cup brown sugar
- 1⅓ cups milk, scalded
- 4 cups pastry flour
- 1 teaspoon cinnamon
- 2 teaspoons baking soda
- ½ teaspoon cloves

Pour hot milk over honey and sugar and stir until dissolved. Sift together the pastry flour, cinnamon, baking soda, and cloves. Stir dry ingredients into liquid mixture. Do not overbeat. Pour into loaf pan lined with wax paper. Bake at 350°F for 1 hour. Cool upside down on rack before removing wax paper.

Easy Cinnamon Bread

Makes 2 loaves

- 1 cup butter, softened
- 2 cups sugar
- 2 eggs
- 2 cups buttermilk or 2 cups milk plus 2 tablespoons vinegar or lemon juice
- 4 cups flour
- 2 teaspoons baking soda

Cinnamon/sugar mixture:

- ⅔ cup sugar
- 2 teaspoons cinnamon

Cream together butter, 2 cups of sugar, and eggs. Add milk, flour, and baking soda. Put ½ of batter (or a little less) into 2 greased loaf pans (¼ of batter in each pan). In a separate bowl, mix ⅔ cups sugar and cinnamon. Sprinkle ¾ of the cinnamon mixture on top of the batter in each pan. Add remaining batter to pans; sprinkle with last of cinnamon mixture. Swirl with a knife. Bake at 350°F for 45–50 minutes or until toothpick tester comes out clean. Cool in pan for 20 minutes before removing. The bread freezes very nicely. This recipe can also be used to make muffins.

English Muffin Bread

- 5 cups flour, divided
- 2 packages yeast
- 1 tablespoon sugar
- 2 teaspoons salt
- ¼ teaspoon baking soda
- 2 cups warm milk
- 1 cup water
- Cornmeal

Combine 2 cups flour, yeast, sugar, salt, and baking soda. Add the milk and water. Beat on low for 30 seconds and then beat on high for 3 minutes. Stir in remaining flour. It is a stiff batter; do not knead. Grease 2 loaf pans well and sprinkle with cornmeal. Spoon batter into pans. Sprinkle cornmeal on top. Cover and let rise until double, about 45 minutes. Bake at 375°F for 35 minutes. Remove from pans immediately.

 Tip: The best way to eat this bread is toasted, just like you would a store-bought English muffin. It freezes nicely, making it easy to keep on hand for unexpected overnight guests who will no doubt rave about your delicious homemade English muffin bread.

Farm Bread

Makes 3 large loaves
- 4 cups scalded milk, cooled
- 2 cups uncooked rolled oats
- 2½ tablespoons soft shortening
- 2 packages yeast
- 1 teaspoon sugar
- ¼ teaspoon ginger
- ½ cup warm water
- ⅔ cup molasses
- 1 tablespoon salt
- 2 cups whole wheat flour
- About 7½ cups white flour
- 1 egg white

Place milk, oats, and shortening in a bowl. Mix and let stand 1 hour at room temperature. Dissolve yeast, sugar, and ginger in the warm water. Let stand 8 minutes or until bubbly. Stir yeast mixture, molasses, and salt into oat mixture. Stir in whole wheat flour and enough of the white flour to make a dough that is easy to handle.

Knead dough 8 minutes. Let rise in greased bowl for 1 ½ hours and punch down. Knead 10 minutes more. Return to bowl. Let rise 45 minutes or until double and punch down. Divide into thirds and shape into loaves. Let rise 45 minutes on greased baking sheet or in loaf pans. Brush tops of loaves with egg white and sprinkle with rolled oats. Bake at 325°F for 45 minutes.

Honey Whole Wheat Bread

Makes 2 loaves
- 2 packages active dry yeast
- 2¼ cups warm water (105°F–115°F), divided
- ⅓ cup honey
- ¼ cup shortening
- 1 tablespoon salt
- 3 cups whole wheat flour
- 3–4 cups white flour

Photo courtesy of The Gray Boxwood, www.thegrayboxwood.com

Dissolve yeast in ½ cup warm water in a large mixing bowl. Stir in honey, shortening, salt, 1¾ cups warm water, and the whole wheat flour. Beat until smooth. Mix in enough white flour to make a dough that's easy to handle. Turn dough onto lightly floured surface. Knead about 10 minutes. Place in greased bowl. Cover and let rise in warm place until double (about 1 hour). Punch down and divide dough in half. Form 2 loaves and place in greased baking pans. Let rise until double (about 1 hour). Bake at 375°F for 40–45 minutes or until loaves are golden brown and sound hollow when tapped. Remove from pans and cool.

Refrigerator Rolls

Makes 48 rolls
- 1½ cups milk
- 1 cup butter or margarine
- ½ cup sugar
- 1 teaspoon salt
- 3 eggs
- 1 package dry yeast
- 2 teaspoons sugar
- ⅛ cup lukewarm water
- 5–5½ cups flour
- Softened butter

Scald milk. Stir in the 1 cup butter, the ½ cup sugar, and the salt. Cool. Add eggs one at a time to milk mixture. Dissolve yeast and the 2 teaspoons sugar in the lukewarm water. Add yeast mixture, then flour, to milk mixture. Beat well. Let rise until double. Punch down and place in refrigerator overnight. The next day, divide dough into 3 parts. Roll each part into a round, as for piecrust. Spread with a little softened butter. Cut each round into 16 wedges. Roll up each wedge from wide end to pointed end. Let rolls rise on a greased pan until light (about 1½ hours). Bake at 375°F for 10–15 minutes.

Sesame Multigrain Bread

Makes 4 large and 4 small loaves

- 6 cups warm water
- 1 cup honey
- 3 heaping tablespoons yeast
- 2 cups rye flour
- 1 cup oatmeal
- 1 cup milk powder
- 3–4 cups whole wheat flour
- 3 tablespoons salt
- 1 scant cup vegetable oil
- 1 cup sesame seeds
- ½–¾ cup sunflower seeds
- ½ cup millet **(optional)**
- Unbleached white flour

Combine warm water, honey, and yeast in a large mixing bowl. Let set. When frothy, add rye flour, oatmeal, milk powder, and enough of the whole wheat flour to make a batter. Cover with plastic wrap and let rise until it reaches top of bowl (about 20–30 minutes). Stir down and add salt, oil, sesame and sunflower seeds, and millet. Stir or work in enough unbleached white flour to make a dough. Knead for 5–10 minutes or until dough has a good texture. Let dough rise and punch down. Let it rise again and punch down. Form into loaves to fit four 9 ½ x 5-inch pans plus four 6 x 3-inch pans. Bake at 350°F–375°F (mini-loaves for 25–30 minutes, large loaves for 30–35 minutes).

Tip: To check whether bread dough has risen sufficiently, press two fingertips into the dough; if a dent remains, the dough is ready for the oven.

White Bread

- 2 cups milk
- 4 tablespoons sugar
- 2 tablespoons salt
- 4 tablespoons shortening
- 1 cup lukewarm water
- 1 teaspoon sugar
- 1 package yeast
- 2 eggs, beaten
- 2 cups cold potato water
- 14 cups all-purpose flour
- Melted butter

Scald the milk. Add the 4 tablespoons of sugar, salt, and shortening. Stir until all is dissolved. In a separate bowl, combine the warm water and the teaspoon of sugar. Stir to dissolve. Sprinkle with the yeast and let stand 10 minutes. Beat with a fork and add to first milk mixture. Add the eggs and potato water. Stir in 4 cups of the flour and beat well. Work in the remaining flour and knead 200 times. Let rise in a warm place until double. Work down and let rise again. Shape into loaves and let rise again. Bake at 275°F for 1 hour. Brush hot loaves with melted butter.

Zwiebach

- 2 cups milk, scalded
- ½ cup butter, softened
- 1 package active dry yeast
- ½ cup lukewarm water
- 2 teaspoons salt
- 2 tablespoons sugar
- 5¾–6 cups flour

What is Potato Water?

Potato water refers to water in which potatoes have been boiled. After boiling, some of the starch from the potatoes is left behind in the water. This water is often called for in bread recipes because it makes the bread incredibly moist. It can also replace milk in a bread recipe. Make potato water by boiling several peeled and cubed potatoes for 20 minutes. Let the water temperature come down before you use it.

Dissolve yeast in lukewarm water and sugar. Scald milk and allow to cool. In a large bowl, combine milk, butter, yeast mixture, and salt. Gradually add 3 cups sifted flour and beat with electric mixer for 5 minutes. Gradually add another 2¾–3 cups flour. Knead until smooth and elastic (about 8–10 minutes). Place in a greased bowl, cover, and let rise until double in bulk. Punch down.

To form zwiebach buns, pinch off small balls of dough the size of a small egg. Place these 1 inch apart on a greased pan. Put a slightly smaller ball on top of the bottom ball. Press down with thumb. Cover and let rise until double in size. Bake at 400°F for 15–20 minutes or until nicely browned. To toast zwiebach, preheat oven to 300°F. Slice each roll lengthwise into ½-inch-thick slices. Arrange slices in a single layer on a baking sheet. Bake at 300°F for 20 minutes or until lightly browned; turn slices over and bake an additional 5 minutes or until crisp. Remove from pan; cool on wire racks.

Butterhorns

- 1 cup milk, scalded
- ½ cup shortening
- ½ cup sugar
- 1 teaspoon salt
- 1 package yeast
- 3 eggs, beaten
- 4½ cups flour
- Melted butter

Heat milk; add shortening, sugar, and salt. Cool to lukewarm, add yeast, and stir. Add eggs and then flour. Knead lightly on a floured surface. Put dough into a greased bowl, cover, and let rise until doubled. Divide into 3 parts and roll each into a circle; brush with melted butter. Cut into 12 pie-shaped wedges. Roll up each wedge starting from the wide end, making a crescent shape. Put on greased pans, cover, and let rise until very light. Bake at 350°F for 10–12 minutes until lightly browned; watch carefully so they do not overbake. Remove from oven and brush tops with butter.

Photo courtesy of The Gray Boxwood, www.thegrayboxwood.com

 Tip: The soft, light texture of these dinner rolls makes them melt-in-your-mouth delicious. Your family will be asking you to make them for all of your family gatherings.

Homemade Hamburger Buns

- 1 package yeast
- ¼ cup warm water
- 1 cup milk
- 2 tablespoons sugar
- 2 heaping tablespoons shortening
- 1 teaspoon salt
- 1 egg, beaten
- 3–3½ cups flour

Dissolve yeast in water. Heat milk. Add sugar, shortening, and salt to milk; cool slightly. Add egg and then yeast and flour. Let rise until doubled. Roll out dough to ½-inch thick. Cut circles with a large round cookie cutter (a 15.5-ounce can works well, too). Place on a 10 x 15-inch baking pan, 12 buns to a pan. You'll need a little space between each bun for rising. Let rise until light. Bake at 400°F for 10–12 minutes or until lightly browned.

Tip: Homemade buns are not what you typically think of when you have a hamburger fry, but these will not disappoint. A freshly grilled burger is always good, but with one of these freshly baked buns, it will be scrumptious.

Raisin Rye Bread

Makes 2 large loaves and 1 small loaf

- 2 packages dry yeast
- 1 teaspoon sugar
- ¼ cup warm water
- 2 cups milk
- 1 tablespoon salt
- ¼ cup oil
- ¼ cup brown sugar
- ¼ cup molasses
- 2 cups rye flour
- 5 cups white flour, divided
- 1 cup raisins
- ⅔ cup water

Dissolve yeast in warm water. Simmer raisins in water until tender. Scald the milk; add salt, oil, sugar, and molasses. Add dissolved yeast, raisins, and the water. Add 2 cups rye flour and 2 cups white flour. Add additional white flour to make a stiff dough (about 5 or more cups). Let rise in bowl until doubled in size (about 2 hours). Shape and put into loaf pans. Let dough rise again. Bake at 375°F for 25–30 minutes.

Tip: To prevent dough from forming a crust while rising in a bowl, first grease the bowl and press the dough into it. Then, turn over the dough, greased side up, and cover it lightly with a dish towel.

Basic Sweet Dough

- 1½ cups milk
- ¼ cup plus 1 tablespoon white sugar, divided
- 2¼ teaspoons salt
- ¾ cup shortening
- ¾ cup lukewarm water
- 3 envelopes yeast (3 tablespoons)
- 3 eggs, well beaten
- 7 cups all-purpose flour, divided

Scald the milk. Add ¼ cup white sugar, salt, and shortening. Stir to dissolve and cool to lukewarm. Measure the lukewarm water and 1 tablespoon of white sugar into a large bowl. Stir until dissolved. Sprinkle with yeast. Let stand 10 minutes. Beat with fork. Stir yeast mixture into milk mixture. Add eggs. Stir in 4 cups all-purpose flour and beat until smooth and elastic. Work in about 3 more cups flour. Turn on slightly floured board and knead lightly until smooth (about 5 minutes). Place in a greased bowl and lightly grease top of dough. Let rise in warm place free from drafts until double in bulk (about 1½ hours).

Use this Basic Sweet Dough recipe to make the Cinnamon Rolls (page 107).

Applesauce Nut Bread

- 1½ cups flour
- 1 teaspoon baking powder
- 1 teaspoon baking soda
- 1 teaspoon salt
- 1 teaspoon cinnamon
- ½ teaspoon nutmeg
- 1 cup oatmeal
- 1 cup chopped walnuts
- ½ cup raisins
- ⅓ cup shortening
- ½ cup brown sugar
- 2 eggs
- 1 cup unsweetened applesauce
- ½ cup milk

Sift together the flour, baking powder, baking soda, salt, cinnamon, and nutmeg into a mixing bowl. Stir in the oatmeal, walnuts, and raisins. Cream the shortening and brown sugar together. Add the eggs and beat until light and fluffy. Blend in the applesauce and milk. Add this creamed mixture to the dry ingredients and beat 30 seconds. (Do not overbeat or batter can become lumpy.) Bake at 350°F for 50–60 minutes.

Tip: Chop nuts the easy way—put them between layers of wax paper and roll with a rolling pin.

Banana Nut Bread

- ⅔ cup shortening
- 2½ cups sifted cake flour
- 1⅔ cups sugar
- 1¼ teaspoons baking powder
- 1 teaspoon baking soda
- 1 teaspoon salt
- 1¼ cups mashed very ripe banana
- ⅔ cup buttermilk, divided
- 2 eggs
- ⅔ cup chopped walnuts

Stir shortening to soften. Sift dry ingredients into same bowl. Add bananas and half of buttermilk. Mix until all flour is dampened. Beat vigorously for 2 minutes. Add remaining buttermilk and eggs and beat 2 minutes longer. Fold in slightly floured nuts. Bake in 2 wax-paper-lined, lightly greased loaf pans. Bake at 350°F for 35 minutes. Can also be baked in 8-inch square cake pan or as cupcakes.

Cinnamon Bread

Makes 4 loaves
- 2–3 packages yeast
- 1 cup warm water
- ½ cup (1 stick) margarine
- 1⅓ cups powdered milk
- 2 teaspoons salt
- 4 cups hot water
- 12 cups flour, divided
- 1⅔ cups plus 1 tablespoon sugar, divided
- 4 teaspoons cinnamon

Tip: If you allow bread to cool in the baking pan, its bottom and sides will get soggy. Cool bread on a rack instead.

Dissolve yeast and 1 tablespoon sugar in the warm water. Stir and set aside. Measure the margarine, ⅔ cup sugar, powdered milk, and salt into a bowl. Add the hot water, stirring until margarine is melted. Stir in 6 cups of the flour. Add the yeast mixture. Gradually add at least 6 cups more flour to make a dough that is easy to knead.

Turn dough onto floured board and knead at least 100 times. Put into bowl and seal. Set aside in warm place for about 1 ½ hours until doubled in bulk. Punch down and divide into 4 parts. Let rest 10 minutes. Mix 1 cup sugar with the cinnamon. Roll each portion of dough into a 7 x 15-inch rectangle. Brush lightly with water. Sprinkle ¼ cup of the cinnamon-sugar mixture over the dough. Roll up as for a jelly roll. Moisten edge and seal. Place in a well-greased pan. Repeat with the other three portions. Let rise in a warm place until loaves reach just above top of pans. Bake at 350°F for 35–40 minutes.

God gives us the ingredients for our daily bread, but He expects us to do the baking!

Pumpkin Bread

Photo courtesy of The Gray Boxwood, www.thegrayboxwood.com

Makes 2 loaves
- 3½ cups flour
- ½ teaspoon baking soda
- 2 teaspoons baking powder
- 1½ teaspoons salt
- 1 teaspoon cinnamon
- ½ teaspoon cloves
- 4 eggs, beaten
- 2⅔ cups sugar
- 2 cups cooked pumpkin
- ⅔ cup water
- ½ cup vegetable oil
- ⅔ cup raisins
- ⅔ cup chopped walnuts
  or other nuts **(optional)**

Sift together first 6 (dry) ingredients. Add sugar, pumpkin, water, and oil to beaten eggs. Mix well. Add liquid ingredients to dry ingredients. Mix until dry ingredients are well moistened. Fold in raisins and nuts. Pour batter into 2 greased 9 x 5-inch loaf pans. Bake at 350°F for 1 hour or until tester inserted in loaves comes out clean. Wrap and store loaves for 24 hours before serving.

Tip: This bread freezes nicely. It is especially nice to bake ahead and have on hand for holiday meals.

Rhubarb Bread

Makes 2 loaves
- 1½ cups white sugar
- ⅔ cup vegetable oil
- 1 egg
- 1 cup buttermilk
- 1 teaspoon vanilla
- 2½ cups flour
- 1 teaspoon baking soda
- 1 teaspoon salt
- 1½ cups diced rhubarb
- ½ cup chopped nuts
  or 1 cup washed and drained raisins
- ½ cup sugar mixed with
  a dash of cinnamon
- 1 tablespoon butter, melted

Combine the 1 ½ cups sugar, oil, egg, buttermilk, and vanilla in a mixing bowl. Mix well. Sift together flour, baking soda, and salt. Add to liquid mixture. Stir in rhubarb and nuts or raisins. Pour batter into 2 greased loaf pans. Sprinkle with the sugar-cinnamon mixture. Drizzle with melted butter. Bake at 325°F for 1 hour. Remove loaves from pans and brush with butter. Sprinkle with a mixture of sugar and cinnamon.

Sour Cream Coffee Cake

- ½ cup shortening
- 1 cup sugar
- 2 eggs
- 1 teaspoon vanilla
- 2 cups flour
- 1 teaspoon baking powder
- 1 teaspoon baking soda
- ½ teaspoon salt
- 1 cup sour cream

Topping:
- 1 cup chopped pecans or walnuts
- ½ cup butter, melted
- ¼ cup white sugar
- ⅓ cup brown sugar
- 1 teaspoon cinnamon

Mix ingredients for topping and set aside. Cream shortening and sugar. Beat in eggs and vanilla. Mix dry ingredients and alternately add the batter (half at a time) with 1 cup sour cream (half at a time). Put half the topping in a greased tube pan. Add half the batter. Repeat. Bake at 350°F for 45 minutes or until done. Let cool for 5 minutes before turning out on a rack.

> *Sorry, we can't come to the door right now. Please leave a message. Don't wait for the beep; there is none.*
>
> —**Sign on the door of an Amish shop**

Funnel Cakes

- 4 eggs
- 3 cups milk
- ¼ cup sugar
- 4 cups flour
- 4 teaspoons baking powder
- 2 teaspoons salt
- Vegetable oil for frying
- Powdered sugar

Beat eggs. Add milk and sugar. Sift dry ingredients together. Add to egg-milk mixture. Beat with a wire whisk until smooth. Heat oil to 375°F. Pour ½ cup batter through funnel into heated oil. Fry a couple of minutes on each side. Drain on paper towels and sprinkle with powdered sugar before serving.

Roll Kuchen

- 3 eggs
- ¾ cup sweet cream
- ¼ cup sweet milk
- 1 teaspoon salt
- ½ teaspoon baking powder
- About 4 cups flour
  (enough to make a soft dough)
- Vegetable oil for frying

Put all ingredients (except flour) into a large bowl. Stir in enough flour to form a soft dough. Knead on a lightly floured surface. Roll out dough. For crisp roll kuchen, roll very thin. For puffy ones, roll about ¼-inch thick. Cut dough into squares or oblong pieces. Fry in hot oil (375°F) until brown.

Soft Pretzels

- 1 envelope yeast
- 5¼ cups water, divided
- 1 teaspoon sugar
- 2 teaspoons salt
- 4–5 cups flour
- Butter as needed
- 4 teaspoons baking soda
- Coarse salt for sprinkling

Dissolve yeast in ¼ cup warm water. Stir in an additional cup of warm water and the sugar. Pour yeast mixture into a bowl. Add salt. Beat in flour to make a stiff dough. Knead for 10 minutes (or until dough is elastic). Place in bowl and spread with butter. Cover. Let rise 45 minutes or until double. Shape in sticks or twists, making the sticks half the thickness of desired pretzel.

Bring 4 cups water to a boil with baking soda. Drop 3 pretzels in at a time. Boil 1 minute or until they float. Remove and drain. Place on buttered cookie sheets. Sprinkle with coarse salt. Bake at 475°F for 12 minutes or until golden brown. To make pretzels crisp, lay them on a cookie sheet and place them in a warm oven set at 200°F for 2 hours. From *Amish Cooking*, published by Pathway Publishers Corporation.

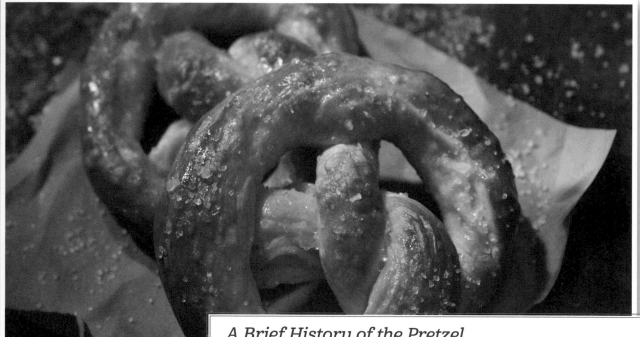

A Brief History of the Pretzel

It has been recorded that monks in the regions near southern France and northern Italy used scraps of dough as a reward for children who did well in their studies and who said their prayers. The pieces of dough were folded in such a way that they resembled a child's arms folded in prayer. The three holes left in the dough were meant to represent the Christian Holy Trinity. The snacks were known as pretiola, *or "little reward." The pretzel would later grow to be a symbol of luck and prosperity, and its form was sometimes incorporated into the architectural details of buildings. The Pennsylvania Dutch brought pretzels to America in 1710. German children wore the pretzels around their necks on New Year's for good luck.*

Grandma's Granola

- 4 cups oatmeal (old fashioned or quick)
- 2½ cups Rice Krispies cereal
- ¾ cup sliced almonds
- 1 cup flaked coconut
- ¼ cup flax meal or wheat germ **(optional)**
- ½ cup honey
- ⅓ cup oil
- 2 tablespoons brown sugar
- 1 teaspoon cinnamon
- 1 teaspoon vanilla

There is only one way to be happy, and that is to make somebody else so.

Combine dry ingredients in a large bowl and set aside. Heat honey, oil, and brown sugar together slowly; do not boil. Remove from heat and stir in vanilla and cinnamon. Pour over dry ingredients. Spread on a 10x15-inch baking sheet lined with parchment paper.

Bake at 325°F for 20–25 minutes. Set timer and stir every 7–8 minutes. Remove when light golden brown. Let cool on pan; store in airtight container. The granola keeps for a long time in the freezer if you choose to make a large batch.

Baked Oatmeal

- ⅓ cup oil
- ½ cup sugar
- 1 large egg, beaten
- 1½ teaspoons baking powder
- ½ teaspoon salt
- ¾ cup milk
- 2 cups quick oats

Photo courtesy of The Gray Boxwood, www.thegrayboxwood.com

Thoroughly mix together all ingredients except the oats. Stir in oats. Pour into a greased 9 x 5-inch pan. Bake at 350°F for 25–30 minutes. This recipe is easily doubled or tripled for a large group.

Breakfast Raisin Bars

Filling:
- 2½ cups raisins
- ½ cup sugar
- 2 tablespoons cornstarch
- ¾ cup water (from cooked raisins)
- 1½ tablespoons lemon juice

Crumb bottom/topping:
- ¾ cup butter, softened
- 1 cup brown sugar
- 1 cup flour
- ½ teaspoon salt
- ½ teaspoon baking soda
- 1½ cups oatmeal

In a saucepan, cover raisins with water and steam for 10 minutes. Pour off water, saving ¾ cup. Combine sugar, cornstarch, raisin water, and lemon juice. Put in saucepan with raisins; cook until thick. Set aside.

Beat butter and brown sugar. Combine flour, salt, baking soda, and oatmeal; blend into butter. Makes a crumbly mixture. Press half the crumbs into a greased 9 x 13-inch baking pan. Spread the filling on top. Pat on remaining crumbs. Bake at 350°F for 25–30 minutes or until golden brown. Keep refrigerated.

Tip: These are such moist and delicious bars, even people who do not normally like raisins will enjoy them. Don't limit yourself to making them for breakfast. They make a great snack bar as well.

Apple Fritters

- 2 cups all-purpose flour
- 2 tablespoons sugar
- 1 teaspoon salt
- 3 teaspoons baking powder
- 2 eggs
- Milk
- Apples, sliced into rings

Sift together the flour, sugar, salt, and baking powder. Beat the eggs slightly in a 2-cup measuring cup. Add milk to the 2-cup level. Beat together with the dry ingredients using beater (blender works, too). Dip apple rings in batter. Fry in deep fat at 375°F (electric fry pan works well).

Cinnamon Rolls

- ¼ Basic Sweet Dough (98)
- Melted butter
- ½ cup brown sugar
- 2 teaspoons cinnamon

Take ¼ of Basic Sweet Dough (98) and roll into 9 x 12-inch rectangle. Brush with melted butter. Sprinkle with brown sugar and cinnamon. Roll up tightly, beginning at wide side. Seal edge well. Cut into 12 slices and place in well-greased rectangle pan. Let rise until double. Bake at 350°F for 30 minutes.

Easy Scones

Makes 12 scones
- 2 cups flour
- 4 teaspoons baking powder
- 2 teaspoons sugar
- ⅓ cup milk or cream
- ½ teaspoon salt
- 4 tablespoons butter or margarine
- 2 eggs
- 1 teaspoon water
- Sugar for sprinkling

Sift dry ingredients. Work in butter with pastry mixer or fork. Add milk and well-beaten eggs (reserve a small amount of unbeaten egg white). Toss on floured board. Pat and roll ¾-inch thick. Cut in squares, diamonds, or triangles. Brush with reserved egg white diluted with 1 teaspoon water. Sprinkle with sugar and bake for 15 minutes at 450°F.

Doughnuts

- 2 packages yeast
- ¾ cup warm water
- 2 tablespoons sugar
- ⅔ cup milk
- 6 tablespoons butter
- ½ cup sugar
- 1¼ teaspoons salt
- 3 eggs, beaten
- 6 cups flour

Glaze:

- 1 pound powdered sugar
- 1 tablespoon cornstarch
- 1 tablespoon cream
- 1 tablespoon butter
- 1 teaspoon vanilla
- Hot water

Dissolve yeast in warm water and set aside. Scald milk. When cool, mix with beaten eggs, salt, sugar, and yeast. Add flour and butter to make a soft dough. Let rise in warm place until double in size. In the meantime, mix glaze ingredients together. Add enough hot water to make a thin glaze; set aside. Roll out dough and cut into doughnuts. Let rise again until light and puffy. Fry in hot oil (365°F). Dip in glaze while warm.

We are not promised skies always blue,
but a Helper to see us through.

Relief Sale Doughnuts

- 1 package yeast dissolved in 1 cup warm water
- 1 cup mashed potatoes
- 1 cup lard
- 1 cup scalded milk
- ½ cup sugar
- 2 eggs
- Flour

Syrup:

- 1 pound powdered sugar
- ½ cup water

Photo courtesy of Discover Lancaster

Mix in order given, adding enough flour so dough will not stick to fingers. Let rise until double in bulk. Roll out and cut. Put on trays sprinkled with flour. Let rise again, fry, and drain. Dry and dip in syrup while still hot.

Banana Bran Muffins

- 1 cup mashed ripe bananas
- ¾ cup milk
- 1½ cups bran cereal
- ½ cup whole wheat flour
- ¾ cup white flour
- ¼ cup sugar
- 3 teaspoons baking powder
- 1 egg
- ¼ cup oil

Combine mashed bananas, milk, egg, oil, and bran cereal; let stand for 5–10 minutes. Whisk dry ingredients together. Stir into banana mixture until moistened. Spoon into paper muffin cups. Bake at 375°F for 12–15 minutes.

Blueberry Muffins

- 2 eggs
- 1 cup milk
- ½ cup butter, melted
- 1 teaspoon vanilla
- 2 cups flour
- ⅔ cup sugar
- 1 tablespoon baking powder
- ½ teaspoon salt
- 2 cups fresh or frozen blueberries
- Melted butter for brushing tops
- Sugar for sprinkling

Beat eggs. Blend in milk, melted butter, and vanilla. Combine dry ingredients. Blend into butter mixture until moistened. Fold in blueberries. (If using frozen berries, rinse and pat dry before adding to batter.) Fill greased or paper-lined muffin cups ⅔ full. Bake at 375°F for 20–25 minutes. Brush tops with melted butter and sprinkle with sugar.

Lemon Poppy Seed Muffins

- 2 cups flour
- 3 teaspoons poppy seeds
- ½ teaspoon salt
- ¼ teaspoon baking soda
- 1 cup sugar
- ½ cup butter
- 2 eggs
- 1 cup lemon yogurt
- 1 teaspoon lemon extract

Stir together flour, poppy seeds, salt, and baking soda. In a large bowl, cream sugar and butter. Beat in the eggs one at a time. Beat in yogurt and lemon extract. Stir in flour mixture until moistened. Spoon into paper muffin cups. Bake at 400°F for 15–20 minutes.

 Tip: When making muffins, you can prevent burning by filling one of the pan's cups with water rather than batter.

Morning Glory Muffins

Makes 14 large muffins
- 2 cups flour
- 1¼ cups white sugar
- 2 teaspoons baking soda
- 2 teaspoons cinnamon
- ½ teaspoon salt
- 3 eggs, beaten
- 1 cup vegetable oil
- 2 teaspoons vanilla
- 2 cups grated carrots
- ½ cup raisins
- ½ cup coconut
- ½ cup chopped nuts
- 1 apple, shredded

Combine flour, sugar, baking soda, cinnamon, and salt. Mix thoroughly. Beat together eggs, oil, and vanilla. Blend into flour mixture. Fold in carrots, raisins, coconut, nuts, and shredded apple. Bake at 350°F for 20 minutes or until tester comes out clean.

 It's nice to have money to buy the things that money can buy, but it's better not to lose the things money cannot buy.

Whole Wheat Muffins

- 1 cup whole wheat flour
- 1 cup white flour
- 1 teaspoon baking soda
- ¼ cup brown sugar
- ¼ teaspoon salt
- 1 cup buttermilk or sour milk
- 3 tablespoons oil
- ½ cup raisins
- 1 egg, beaten

Combine dry ingredients. Make a well and add liquid ingredients. Stir only until blended. Fill greased muffin tins half full with batter. Bake at 375°F for 15 minutes.

Apple Pancakes

Serves 2
- 2 apples
- 3 tablespoons flour
- 1 egg
- Pinch of salt
- Enough whole milk to make batter a little thicker than cream (¼–⅓ cup)

Chop 2 apples. Fry in a covered pan to cook. Combine all other ingredients (except flour) to create a thin batter that will spread over the entire pan. Cut in flour and turn as best you can.

Tip: To reheat pancakes without overcooking them, wrap them in a dish towel and put them in a 250°F oven for a few minutes.

Buckwheat Pancakes

- 1 cup white flour
- ½ cup whole wheat flour
- 1 cup buckwheat flour
- 5 heaping tablespoons sugar
- 2 teaspoons salt
- 1 package dry yeast
- 2 cups warm water
- ⅓ cup baking soda dissolved in a bit of warm water

Mix flours, sugar, and salt in a large bowl. Mix the yeast with the warm water. Mix into the dry ingredients. Let batter rise, covered, for 2 hours. Mix the baking soda water into the batter just before frying.

Tip: You can speed up the chore of cutting up pancakes for small children by using a pizza cutter. Even a stack is easy to cut this way!

Buttermilk Pancakes

- 2 cups buttermilk
- 2 cups flour
- 3 tablespoons butter, melted
- 1 teaspoon baking powder
- ½ teaspoon salt
- 1 teaspoon baking soda
- 2 teaspoons sugar
- 2 eggs, separated

Sift dry ingredients. Add buttermilk and beat until smooth. Add egg yolks and melted butter. Fold in beaten egg whites. Bake on hot, slightly greased griddle until golden brown.

Griddle Cakes

- 1 egg
- 1 cup milk
- ½ teaspoon salt
- 1 cup bread flour
- 2 teaspoons baking powder
- 1½ tablespoons melted shortening

Beat egg and add milk. Sift flour with baking powder and salt. Beat into mixture. Add shortening. Drop by tablespoon on hot griddle and brown on both sides. Serve with maple syrup.

Russian Pancakes

- 5 eggs
- 1 tablespoon sugar
- 2 teaspoons salt
- ½ cup (1 stick) margarine, melted
- 6 cups milk, divided
- 4 cups flour, divided

Beat eggs. Add sugar, salt, and margarine. Mix. Add two-thirds of the milk and half the flour. Mix well. Add remaining milk and flour. Mix again. Pour batter into hot, greased pan. Lift and tilt pan so that batter covers bottom. Brown pancake lightly on first side. Flip to other side and brown.

Russian Pancakes

These pancakes were a favorite of Germans living in Russia who later emigrated to the United States. Traditionally, a filling was added to the pancakes, which were then rolled up and eaten with a fork.

Living the Simple Life

Top Ten Amish Men's Names

10. Mervin
9. Eli
8. Vernon
7. Jacob
6. Wayne
5. Elmer
4. John
3. Leroy
2. Amos
1. Samuel

Top Ten Amish Surnames

10. Fisher
9. Graber
8. King
7. Bontrager
6. Troyer
5. Schwartz
4. Beiler
3. Yoder
2. Stoltzfus
1. Miller

Whole Wheat Pancakes

Makes 8–10 pancakes
- 2 eggs
- 1 cup brown sugar
- ½ teaspoon salt
- 2 teaspoons baking powder
- 1 cup milk
- 2 cups whole wheat flour
- Melted shortening

Beat eggs. Add sugar and milk. Sift dry ingredients and add to liquid. Add melted shortening and blend together. Bake on hot, lightly greased griddle or pan.

Breakfast Casserole

- 1 pound fried bacon, chopped
- 1 medium onion, chopped
- 6 eggs, lightly beaten
- 4 cups frozen, shredded hash brown potatoes, thawed
- 2 cups shredded cheddar cheese
- 1½ cups small curd cottage cheese
- 1¼ cups shredded Swiss cheese

In a large skillet, cook bacon and onion until bacon is crisp. Drain. In a bowl, combine the remaining ingredients; stir in bacon mixture. Transfer to a greased 9 x 13-inch baking pan. Bake uncovered at 350°F for 30–35 minutes or until set and bubbly. Let stand for 10 minutes before serving.

Hearty Breakfast Casserole

- 1 pound sausage
- ¼ cup butter or margarine, melted
- 6 slices bread
- 1½ cups shredded cheddar cheese
- 5 eggs
- 2 cups half-and-half
- 1 teaspoon dry mustard
- ½ teaspoon salt

Cook sausage. Drain well and set aside. Place melted butter in 13 x 9-inch baking pan. Cut bread into small squares (remove crusts or not, as desired). Spread bread over butter. Spread drained sausage over bread. Cover with cheese. Beat eggs, half-and-half, mustard, and salt together. Pour over ingredients in baking pan. Chill 8 hours or overnight. Bake at 350°F for 40–50 minutes.

Swallowing words before you say them is so much better than having to eat them afterward.

Dried Beef Gravy on Biscuits

Serves 8

- ½ pound dried beef
- 4 tablespoons butter
- 6 tablespoons flour
- 6 cups milk

Melt butter in skillet. Tear the dried beef into small pieces and stir into the butter. Brown meat lightly. Stir in flour. When flour is dissolved into butter, add milk, stirring constantly. Cook over low heat until the mixture thickens. Serve over Baking Powder Biscuits found on page 90.

Canning Recipes

Bread and Butter Pickles

- 8 cups cucumbers, thinly sliced
- 2 sliced onions

Syrup:
- 2 cups sugar
- 2 teaspoons salt
- 2 teaspoons dry mustard
- 2 teaspoons turmeric
- 1 cup water
- 1 cup vinegar

Soak cucumbers and onions in cold water for 3 hours and drain. Combine syrup ingredients. Cook pickles in syrup for several minutes. Place in jars and process in boiling water for 5 minutes.

Photos courtesy of The Gray Boxwood, www.thegrayboxwood.com

Crisp Pickle Slices

- 1 gallon medium cucumbers, sliced quite thin
- ¾ cup pickling salt dissolved in boiling water

Cooking Brine:
- 6 cups water
- 2 cups vinegar
- 1 tablespoon alum
- 1 tablespoon turmeric

Pickling Syrup:
- 1½ cups vinegar
- 1½ cups water
- 6 cups sugar
- 1½ teaspoons dill seed
- 1 tablespoon pickling spice
- 1 tablespoon mustard seed

Cover cucumbers with the boiling water/salt solution. Let stand overnight. Drain and wash the next morning. Combine ingredients for cooking brine. Add cucumbers and simmer 30 minutes. Drain and rinse. Bring pickling syrup ingredients to a boil. Pack cucumber slices in jars. Pour boiling syrup over slices and seal immediately.

Dill Pickle Spears

Soak cucumber spears in ice water for 2 hours and drain. Pack spears into jars. Add a few onion slices and 1 head fresh dill or 1–1½ teaspoons dried dill seed to each jar. Bring syrup ingredients to a boil. Pour boiling syrup over cucumbers in jars and seal. Process in boiling water bath for 10 minutes.

- 4–5 quarts cucumbers, cut into spears
- Ice water
- Onion slices
- Fresh dill heads or dried dill seed

Pickling Syrup:
- 3 cups sugar
- 3 cups water
- 1½ cups vinegar
- 1 tablespoon salt

Tip: When selecting fruit and vegetables for home canning, try to buy them in approximately the same size so they'll cook more evenly before canning.

Favorite Sweet Pickles

- 7 pounds medium cucumbers
- Boiling water to cover
- 1 quart vinegar
- 8 cups sugar
- 2 tablespoons pickling salt
- 2 tablespoons mixed pickling spice

On the first day, wash cucumbers in the morning. Cover them with boiling water. Let stand 8–12 hours. Drain. Drain again in the evening, then cover with fresh boiling water. Repeat the steps from the first day on the second day. On the third day, cut cucumbers into rings ¼-inch thick. Combine vinegar, sugar, salt, and spices. Bring to a boil. Pour over sliced cucumbers. Let stand 24 hours. On the fourth day, drain syrup. Bring to a boil. Pour over cucumbers. Repeat the steps from the fourth day on the fifth day. On the sixth day, drain syrup. Bring to a boil. Add cucumber slices and bring to the boiling point. Pack into hot, sterilized jars. Seal.

Grandma Hannah's Ready-to-Eat Pickles

- 7 cups thinly sliced cucumbers
- 1 tablespoon celery seed
- 1 tablespoon salt
- 1 cup sliced onions
- 1 cup sliced red or green pepper **(optional)**
- 2 cups sugar
- 1 cup vinegar

Sprinkle cucumber slices with celery seed and salt. Let set 30 minutes and drain. Add onions and peppers. Mix together sugar and vinegar. Stir until sugar is dissolved (do not heat). Pour over drained vegetables. Pickles can be eaten immediately or stored in the refrigerator.

One of the most treasured recipes from my own grandmother!

—Carole

Lime Pickles

- 7 pounds cucumbers
- 2 cups hydrated pickling lime
- 2 gallons water
- 9 cups sugar
- 1 teaspoon celery seed
- 1 teaspoon mixed pickling spices
- 1 tablespoon or less pickling salt
- 2 quarts vinegar

Wash cucumbers well. Slice ¼-inch thick. Mix pickling lime and water and pour over slices. Let stand 24 hours. Stir occasionally very carefully with hands. Drain. Wash cucumbers to remove lime residue and soak in clear water for 3–6 hours. Mix together sugar, celery seed, pickling spices, pickling salt, and vinegar. Drain cucumber slices and pour cold vinegar mixture over them. Let stand 12 hours. Boil cucumbers in the vinegar mixture for 35 minutes or until cucumbers begin to appear clear. Put in jars and seal.

Red Cinnamon Pickles

Cover cucumber chunks with a solution of the lime and 2 gallons water. Soak for 24 hours. Drain and rinse well. Soak in cold water for 3 hours and drain. Place cucumbers in a large kettle. Add brine ingredients. Simmer 2 hours. Drain and rinse thoroughly. Mix together syrup ingredients and bring to a boil (be sure candy is dissolved). Pour syrup over drained cucumbers. Let stand overnight. Drain and heat for 3 mornings. On the third morning, pack in jars and seal. Put one cinnamon stick in each jar.

For this recipe, use large cucumbers that have a yellowish color. The lighter-colored flesh will produce a better red color.

Tip: With their brilliant red color, these pickles are a beautiful addition to a condiment plate.

- 2 gallons cucumber chunks
- 2 cups pickling lime
- 2 gallons water

Cooking Brine:
- 1 cup vinegar
- 1 small bottle red food coloring
- 1 tablespoon alum
- Water to cover

Pickling Syrup:
- 4 cups vinegar
- 15 cups sugar
- 2 packages Red Hot cinnamon candies
- 8 sticks cinnamon
- 4 cups water

 Good deeds have echoes.

Sweet-Sour Dill Pickles

- Medium-sized cucumbers
- 12–16 onion slices
- 2 stalks celery, quartered
- 8 heads fresh dill
- 4 cups sugar
- ½ cup pickling salt
- 1 quart vinegar
- 2 cups water

Wash freshly picked cucumbers. Cut into chunks or slices ¼-inch thick (enough to fill 4 clean quart jars). Add 3–4 onion slices, 2 pieces celery, and 2 heads dill to each jar. Dissolve sugar and salt in vinegar and water. Bring to a boil. Pour boiling liquid into jars. Seal at once. Do not use for 30 days.

Sweet Gherkins

Makes 7–8 pints
- 5 quarts (about 7 pounds) small cucumbers (1½–3 inches long)
- ½ cup salt
- 8 cups sugar, divided
- 6 cups vinegar, divided
- ¾ teaspoon turmeric
- 2 teaspoons celery seed
- 2 teaspoons whole mixed pickling spice
- 8 1-inch pieces stick cinnamon
- ½ teaspoon fennel *(optional)*
- 2 teaspoons vanilla *(optional)*

Wash cucumbers thoroughly (stem end may be left on if desired).

First day: In the morning, cover cucumbers with boiling water. Let sit for 6–8 hours. In the afternoon, drain cucumbers and cover with fresh boiling water.

Second day: In the morning, drain cucumbers and cover with fresh boiling water. In the afternoon, drain cucumbers and add salt. Cover with fresh boiling water.

Third day: In the morning, drain cucumbers. Prick each cucumber in several places with a table fork. (You may want to slice thicker ones in half.) Make a syrup of 3 cups of the sugar and 3 cups of the vinegar. Add turmeric and spices (except vanilla). Heat to boiling and pour over cucumbers. (Syrup will only partially cover cucumbers.) In the afternoon, drain syrup into pan. Add 2 cups sugar and 2 cups vinegar and heat. Pour over pickles.

Fourth day: In the morning, drain syrup into pan. Add 2 cups sugar and 1 cup vinegar and heat. Pour over pickles. In the afternoon, drain syrup into pan. Add remaining 1 cup sugar and the vanilla. Heat-pack pickles into pint jars and cover with syrup. Adjust lids. Process for 5 minutes in boiling water bath. Start to count processing time as soon as water returns to boiling.

Chow Chow

- 1 cup chopped bell peppers
- 1 cup chopped cabbage
- 1 whole cucumber, chopped
- 1 cup chopped onion
- 2 quarts water
- ¼ cup salt
- 1 cup chopped carrots
- 1 cup chopped green beans
- 2 teaspoons mustard seed
- 2 teaspoons celery seed
- 2 cups vinegar
- 2 cups sugar

Soak the peppers, cucumber, and onion overnight in water and salt. Drain. Cook carrots and green beans for 10 minutes and drain. Mix all ingredients. Heat to a boil. Pack in jars and seal.

Tip: This relish is a common, everyday side at many Amish meals. It is sometimes referred to as "End of the Season" relish: whatever vegetables are left in the garden are combined together to make this tangy relish.

Pickled Baby Corn

The corn for this recipe must be picked just as the tassels are starting to form and the small cobs are no more than 2 inches long. Field corn is usually used. Husk and remove the silk from cobs. Boil cobs 7 minutes in salt water. Boil syrup made of the vinegar, white sugar, and pickling spices (tied in cloth bag) for 5 minutes. Remove spice bag. Pack hot corncobs in sterile jars. Cover with boiling syrup and seal immediately.

- 6 quarts of small corncobs
- Salt water
- 5 cups vinegar
- 4 cups white sugar
- 2 tablespoons pickling spices

Mutual Aid

Amish and most conservative Mennonites do not purchase insurance as it diminishes reliance on God and their fellow members. This belief is based on the early church as described in **Acts 4:32.**

"All the believers were one in heart and mind. No one claimed that any of their possessions was their own, but they shared everything they had."

Canning Recipes

Canning Recipes 123

Pickled Watermelon Rind

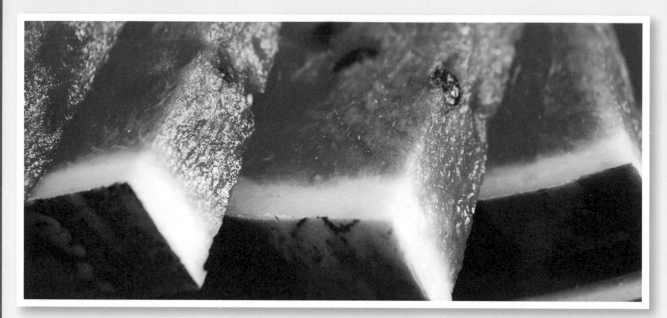

- 9 cups watermelon rind
- 3 tablespoons salt
- 4 cups water
- 4 cups white sugar
- 2 cups white vinegar
- 2 cups water
- 6 cinnamon sticks
- 2 tablespoons whole cloves
- 2 tablespoons whole allspice

To prepare the rind, trim off outer green skin and most of pink flesh, leaving only a bit of pink on white rind. Cut rind into 1½ x 1¾-inch pieces. Soak prepared rind overnight in a brine made of the salt and 4 cups water. In the morning, drain, cover with fresh water, and cook until tender. Heat the sugar, vinegar, and 2 cups water to boiling point. Tie the cinnamon sticks, cloves, and allspice in cloth bag and add. Add cooked rind and simmer until rind is transparent (about 45 minutes). Pack hot rind in sterile jars. Remove spice bag from syrup and bring to boil again. Pour boiling syrup over rind, making sure syrup completely covers rind. Seal jars.

Spiced Crab Apples

- 4 pounds crab apples
- 2 cups vinegar
- 2 cups water
- 2 cups sugar
- 1 tablespoon whole cloves
- 3 cinnamon sticks
- 1 teaspoon whole ginger tied in cheesecloth bag

Wash crab apples and remove blossom ends. Boil the vinegar, water, and sugar together. Add the cloves, cinnamon sticks, and ginger. Add the crab apples. Simmer until tender. Seal in sterile jars.

Spiced Pickled Beets

Photo courtesy of The Gray Boxwood,
www.thegrayboxwood.com

- 10–15 beets (depending on size)
- 2 cups sugar
- 2 cups vinegar
- 2 cups water
- 1 teaspoon ground cloves
- 1 teaspoon ground cinnamon

Trim beet tops down to 1 inch. (Do not cut into beets or color will bleed during cooking.) Wash beets well. Cook in boiling water until tender. Drain and cover with cold water. Slip skins off and trim off tops and roots. Cut beets into quarters or eighths depending on size. (Beets may also be sliced.) Combine remaining ingredients. Bring to a boil. Add beets to syrup and boil 10 minutes. Pack into sterilized jars and seal.

Photo courtesy of Discover Lancaster

Country-Style Hot Dog Relish

- 4 cups sliced cucumbers, not pared, but with seeds removed
- 3 cups roughly chopped onions
- 3 cups roughly chopped cabbage
- 2 cups roughly chopped green tomatoes
- 3 red peppers, cut in chunks
- 3 green peppers, cut in chunks
- ½ cup pickling salt
- 2 tablespoons mustard seed
- 1 tablespoon celery seed
- 1 tablespoon turmeric
- 5 cups sugar
- 4 cups vinegar
- 2 cups cold water

Grind all vegetables using a coarse blade. Drain. Sprinkle with salt and let stand overnight. Drain and rinse well. Combine remaining ingredients and pour over vegetables. Heat to a full boil. Boil 7–10 minutes. Place in hot jars and seal.

Green Hot Dog Relish

- 4 quarts cucumbers
- 1 quart onions
- 2 bunches celery
- 4 red sweet peppers
- 4 green sweet peppers
- ¼ cup salt
- 5 cups white sugar
- 1 quart vinegar
- 5 drops oil of cinnamon (or 1 teaspoon ground cinnamon)
- 5 drops oil of cloves (or ½ teaspoon ground cloves)

Put the first 5 ingredients through a meat chopper. Add the salt and let stand in crock overnight. Add the sugar and vinegar. Boil slowly for 1 hour. When cold, add the oil of cinnamon and oil of cloves. Let stand 2 days at room temperature, stirring occasionally. Heat to boiling point and put in sterile jars.

Cucumber Relish

- 12 cups cucumbers, finely chopped
- 1 quart onions, finely chopped
- 1 large head cauliflower, chopped
- 4 red sweet peppers, chopped
- ¼ cup salt
- 8 cups white sugar
- 3 cups cider vinegar
- 1½ tablespoons mustard
- 2 tablespoons turmeric
- 1½ tablespoons celery seed
- ⅔ cup flour mixed with 1 cup water

Add the salt to the cucumbers, onions, cauliflower, and peppers. Let stand overnight. Next morning, drain well and add the sugar, vinegar, mustard, turmeric, and celery seed. Bring to boil and add the flour, mixed with the 1 cup water. Boil 30 minutes and seal in sterile jars.

Fruit and Tomato Relish

- 6-quart basket peeled tomatoes
- 6 large pears
- 6 large apples
- 6 large peaches
- 4 onions
- 4 cups granulated sugar
- 2 tablespoons salt
- ½ cup pickling spices
- 1 pint vinegar
- Red and green sweet peppers, chopped *(optional)*

Tip: To speed up the ripening of pears, tomatoes, or peaches, put them in a brown paper bag along with a ripe apple. Punch some holes in the bag, and put it in a cool place out of direct sunlight.

Chop fruits and vegetables finely. Add the sugar, salt, pickling spices (tied loosely in a bag), and vinegar. Simmer in large pot for 1 hour, stirring often. Remove spice bag and seal in hot sterile jars. Chopped red and green sweet peppers may also be added.

Chili Sauce

Makes 8 pints

- 7–8 quarts ripe tomatoes
- 2 green peppers, chopped
- 2 red peppers, chopped
- 2 stalks celery, diced
- 3 medium onions, diced
- 1 cup sugar
- 1 cup vinegar
- 2 tablespoons salt
- 2 tablespoons paprika
- 1½ teaspoons each of ground cloves, ground allspice, black pepper, and cinnamon
- ½ teaspoon dry mustard

Cover tomatoes with boiling water to make it easy to slip off skins. Quarter or chop tomatoes and place in a large pot. Add remaining ingredients and cook until thick, stirring occasionally. Pour into hot sterilized jars and seal.

Gooseberry Ketchup

- 4 pounds gooseberries
- 2 pounds white sugar
- ½ pint vinegar
- 1 tablespoon cinnamon
- 1 tablespoon cloves
- 1 teaspoon black pepper
- 1 teaspoon salt

Boil all ingredients together for 30 minutes or until thick. Stir frequently to prevent sticking.

 The person who forgives does more for himself than anyone else.

Homemade Ketchup

- 12½ cups seeded tomatoes
- 2½ cups celery
- 2½ cups onions
- 2 cups cider vinegar, divided
- 4 cups sugar
- 2 tablespoons pickling salt
- 1 tablespoon pickling spice, tied in a cheesecloth bag

Purée the tomatoes in a blender. Purée the celery in a blender with 1 cup of the vinegar. Purée the onion in a blender with the remaining vinegar. Cook the puréed tomatoes, celery, and onion to a "boiled down" consistency. Add the sugar, pickling salt, and pickling spice. Cook to the desired thickness. Put in jars. Seal and process in a water bath for 15 minutes.

The discovery of a new dish makes more for the happiness of man than the discovery of a star.

Tomato Butter

- 12 medium tomatoes
- 1½ cups white sugar
- 2 cups white vinegar
- 1 teaspoon salt
- 1 teaspoon whole cinnamon
- 1 teaspoon cloves

Peel the tomatoes and cut them into small pieces. Add the sugar and boil 1 hour, stirring often to prevent sticking. Add the vinegar, salt, cinnamon, and cloves (tied in bag). Boil until thick.

Jams and Jellies

Black Currant Preserves

- 2 cups black currants
- 4 cups cold water, divided
- 6 cups sugar

Boil the black currants in 2 cups water for 10 minutes. Mash thoroughly. Add 2 more cups water and the sugar. Boil 20 minutes. Seal in sterile jars. Serve on ice cream or with cream.

Tip: Place several marbles in the kettle when you're making jelly, jam, or other foods requiring continuous stirring. The marbles will roll constantly across the bottom of the kettle and prevent sticking. Remove the marbles before pouring the food into jars.

Blueberry Rhubarb Jam

- 5 cups diced rhubarb
- 1 cup water
- 5 cups sugar
- 1 can blueberry pie filling
- 1 6-ounce package raspberry gelatin
- Half a 6-ounce package unflavored gelatin

Cook rhubarb in the water until tender (10 minutes). Add sugar and cook 3 minutes longer, stirring constantly. Add pie filling and cook 8 minutes. Remove from heat. Soften both flavored gelatin and unflavored gelatin in a bit of cold water and add to rhubarb mixture. Stir until gelatin is completely dissolved. Pour into jars and seal.

Tip: When you're making jelly or jam, use a potato masher for stirring. The handle is long enough to keep your hand cool, and the shape prevents the masher from slipping into the pot.

Cider Apple Butter

Wash the apples well. Core, but do not peel. Slice into eighths. Add 4 pounds sugar. Let sit overnight (8–12 hours) until juice forms. Put apples and juice into a pressure cooker. Cook 30 minutes at 10 pounds pressure. Put mixture through a food mill. Stir in 2 cans frozen apple juice and 1 teaspoon cinnamon per gallon of mixture. Put on stove and cook over low heat. Can in pints or quarts.

- 4 gallons (about 20 pounds) Jonathan apples
- 4 pounds sugar (1 pound per gallon of apples)
- 2 12-ounce cans frozen apple juice per gallon
- 1 teaspoon cinnamon per gallon

Photo courtesy of The Gray Boxwood, www.thegrayboxwood.com

Dandelion Jelly

- 1 quart dandelion flowers (best picked in the morning)
- 2 quarts water
- Lemon juice
- Several packages (1¾ ounces each) powdered fruit pectin
- 5½ cups sugar

Rinse the dandelion flowers in cold water and remove stems. Bring flowers to a boil in the 2 quarts water. Boil 3 minutes. Cool and strain, pressing petals with fingers to extract all the juice. You may have to strain the juice several times to remove all small specks. Measure the liquid. Add 2 tablespoons lemon juice and 1 package (1¾ ounces) powdered fruit pectin to every 3 cups of dandelion liquid. Bring to a boil. Add the sugar. Continue stirring. Bring to a boil and boil hard for 2½ minutes. Pour into jars and seal.

Heavenly Jam

- 7 cups rhubarb, chopped
- 6 cups sugar
- 1 20-ounce can pineapple tidbits
- 3 ounces cherry gelatin powder
- 3 ounces pineapple gelatin powder

Combine the rhubarb, sugar, and pineapple tidbits. Boil for 20 minutes. Add the gelatin powders. Stir until dissolved and put into jars. Store in refrigerator.

Tip: Label all your preserved foods with the contents and the date.

Peach Conserve

- 3 pounds (6 cups) ground or chopped peaches
- 6 cups white sugar
- ½ dozen small oranges, ground
- ⅔ cup brown sugar
- ⅔ cup corn syrup

Combine all ingredients and boil together until thick (about 20 minutes). Seal in sterile jars.

 Tip: If canned food smells strange or looks cloudy after opening, discard it immediately without tasting it.

Rhubarb Jam

- 4 cups finely chopped rhubarb
- 4 cups sugar
- 1 cup strawberries
- 1 package strawberry gelatin

Stir rhubarb, sugar, and strawberries in a heavy saucepan until thoroughly mixed. Place on heat, bring to a boil, and boil 15 minutes. Remove from heat. Add gelatin, stirring until dissolved. Seal in sterilized jars. Substitute 1 cup crushed pineapple and 1 package pineapple gelatin for the strawberries and strawberry gelatin to vary recipe. You can also increase the rhubarb to 5 cups and use 1 package of any flavor gelatin.

Strawberry Rhubarb Jam

- 5 cups rhubarb
- 4 cups sugar
- 1 6-ounce package strawberry gelatin

Mix the rhubarb and sugar and let stand overnight. In the morning, boil 5 minutes. Add strawberry gelatin. Seal into sterile jars. Store in refrigerator or cool place.

Photo courtesy of The Gray Boxwood, www.thegrayboxwood.com

Tomato Marmalade

- 4 cups tomatoes, peeled and cut fine
- 4 cups brown sugar
- 1 orange and 1 lemon, shredded very finely

Combine all ingredients and cook until thick (about 20 minutes), stirring frequently.

Living the Simple Life

The Amish incorporate their focus on simplicity and traditional values into their meals. They grow their own food on their own land. What isn't consumed is canned for use over the winter or sold. Many Amish foods are sold at roadside stands and markets, including pies, preserves, produce, desserts, and canned goods.

Zucchini Jam

Makes about 3 pints
- 6 cups peeled and chopped zucchini
- 6 cups sugar
- ¼ cup lemon juice
- 1 cup crushed pineapple
- 1 6-ounce package flavored gelatin (orange, apricot, strawberry, or flavor of choice)

Mix together zucchini and sugar in a large, heavy saucepan. Boil 15 minutes. Add lemon juice and pineapple. Boil 8 minutes. Remove from heat and mix in flavored gelatin. Stir well. Put into jars. Seal with wax, process, or freeze.

Children's Favorite Maple Cream

- 4 cups brown sugar
- 2 tablespoons flour
- 2 teaspoons baking powder
- 1 cup thin cream
- 4 tablespoons butter
- Pinch of salt
- Pecans or walnuts, chopped (*optional*)

Mix ingredients well. Cook, stirring constantly, until mixture reaches the soft ball stage. Add chopped pecans or walnuts if desired. Spread into buttered shallow pan.

> *Put the swing where the children want it. The grass will grow back.*

Chocolate Nut Caramels

Boil together sugar, corn syrup, cocoa, butter, and 1 cup of the cream. Boil until mixture reaches the thread stage. Slowly add the other cup of cream. Boil until mixture reaches the firm ball stage when tested in cold water. Add vanilla and nuts. Beat until creamy.

- 2 cups white sugar
- ½ cup corn syrup
- 2 cups cream, divided
- ½ cup butter or margarine
- 6 tablespoons cocoa
- 1 cup walnuts
- 2 teaspoons vanilla

Living the Simple Life

According to AmishAmerica.com, there are about 300,000 Amish in North America. The 5 largest Amish settlements are: Holmes County, Ohio; Lancaster County, Pennsylvania; Elkhart/LaGrange Counties, Indiana; and Geauga County, Ohio.

Approximately 100,000 Amish live in these communities, with the remaining 200,000 living in 475 much smaller communities in 30 states and Ontario.

Christmas Candy Crispies

- 1 cup sugar
- 1 cup white corn syrup
- 1 cup cream
- 1 cup angel flake coconut
- 1 cup salted peanuts
- 3 cups Rice Krispies cereal
- 3 cups corn flakes, crushed

Cook sugar, syrup, and cream together until it reaches the soft ball stage (235°F–245°F). Stir only until sugar is dissolved. Mix cereals, coconut, and peanuts together. Pour hot syrup over mixture and blend together. Press into buttered 9 x 13-inch pan. Cut into squares when cooled.

Church Windows

- ½ cup butter
- 10 ounces chocolate chips
- 10.5-ounce package colored miniature marshmallows
- Flaked coconut

Melt the butter and chocolate chips in a double boiler or microwave and cool. Add the marshmallows and stir until coated. Divide in half and place onto 2 pieces of waxed paper, sprinkled liberally with the flaked coconut. Roll up jelly roll-style and wrap in waxed paper. Refrigerate. Slice into ¼-inch "windows" right before serving.

Cracker Jack

- 1 small box puffed rice
- ½ pound blanched peanuts
- 1 cup corn syrup
- 1 cup molasses
- 2 cups brown sugar
- 1 tablespoon butter
- 2 tablespoons vinegar
- ½ teaspoon baking soda

Boil all ingredients (except puffed rice and peanuts) until a small amount will form a ball in cold water. Pour mixture over puffed rice and peanuts. Stir until mixed. Form into balls with buttered hands and drop on buttered pans.

Easy Caramels

- 3 cups white sugar
- 1 cup corn syrup
- 1 cup heavy cream
- 1 cup milk
- 2 tablespoons cornstarch
- 4 tablespoons butter
- ½ teaspoon salt
- 1 teaspoon vanilla
- 1 cup nutmeats *(optional)*

Be sure to use a heavy saucepan. Thoroughly mix cornstarch, sugar, corn syrup, milk, cream, butter, and salt. Stir mixture over low heat until sugar is dissolved. Cook until mixture is 248°F or until a few drops are as hard as caramels should be when finished. Stir only occasionally so mixture will not stick to bottom of pan. Remove from heat and let cool a few minutes before adding nuts and vanilla. Pour into buttered pan. When cold, cut and wrap in waxed paper.

 The most beautiful attire is a smile.

Marshmallows

- 2 envelopes unflavored gelatin
- ½ cup cold water
- ½ teaspoon salt
- 2 cups sugar
- 1 teaspoon vanilla
- ¾ cup boiling water
- Powdered sugar
- Coconut or chopped nuts

Boil 2 cups sugar and water together until the mixture reaches the thread stage. Remove from heat. Soften gelatin in cold water. Add to hot syrup and stir until dissolved. Let stand until partly cool, then add salt and flavoring. Beat until mixture becomes thick, fluffy, and soft.

Pour into an 8 x 4-inch pan thickly covered with powdered sugar. Have the mixture 1 inch in depth. Let stand in refrigerator until thoroughly chilled. With a sharp, wet knife, loosen around edges of pan. Turn out on a board and lightly flour with powdered sugar. Cut in squares and roll in confectioners sugar, chopped nuts, or coconut.

From *Amish Cooking*, published by Pathway Publishers Corporation

Munch Mix

- 6 cups Cheerios cereal
- ½ cup sugar
- ¼ cup margarine
- 2 tablespoons corn syrup
- ¼ teaspoon baking soda
- 8 ounces M&Ms

Place Cheerios in a 2-quart glass casserole. Set aside. Combine sugar, margarine, and syrup in a 1-quart glass bowl. Microwave on full power for 2 minutes, stirring once. Microwave again on low (30%) for 3 minutes. Stir in baking soda. Pour syrup over cereal and toss to coat. Microwave on half-power (50%) for 4 minutes. Spread on waxed paper to cool. Add M&Ms.

Peanut Brittle

Photo courtesy of The Gray Boxwood,
www.thegrayboxwood.com

- 2 cups white sugar
- 1 cup corn syrup
- ½ cup water
- 3 cups salted peanuts
- 1 teaspoon butter, melted
- 1 teaspoon baking soda
- 1 teaspoon vanilla

Combine sugar, syrup, and water. Cook until it reaches the hard ball stage. Add peanuts and melted butter. Continue cooking until syrup is a golden brown. Stir during cooking. Remove from heat and add baking soda and vanilla. Beat until baking soda is mixed through syrup. Pour into buttered pans and break into pieces when cold.

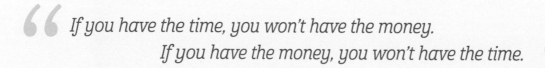 *If you have the time, you won't have the money.*
If you have the money, you won't have the time.

Shanty Candy

- 2 cups granulated sugar
- ¾ cup molasses
- ¼ cup water
- 2 egg whites
- Vanilla to taste
- ½ cup chopped English walnuts
- ½ cup dates

Bring sugar, molasses, and water to a boil. Boil until it reaches hard ball stage on a candy thermometer (or until it is crisp when a small amount is dropped into cold water). While syrup is cooking, beat egg whites until very stiff. When syrup is ready, pour it slowly into beaten whites. Beat candy until too stiff to work, mixing in vanilla, walnuts, and dates just before it stiffens. Pour into buttered pan. Cut into squares before it hardens.

Taffy

- 1 quart white sugar
- 1 pint cream
- 1 tablespoon gelatin dissolved in ¼ cup cold water
- 1 tablespoon paraffin
- 1 pint light corn syrup

Combine all ingredients and boil until it forms a hard ball in cold water when dropped from a tablespoon (250°F on candy thermometer). Pour onto a well-greased cookie sheet. When cool enough to handle, start pulling. When an ivory color is obtained, pull into a long, thin rope and cut with kitchen scissors.

From *Amish Cooking*, published by Pathway Publishers Corporation.

Best-Ever Chocolate Chip Cookies

- ½ cup solid vegetable shortening
- ½ cup (1 stick) margarine
- 1 cup brown sugar
- ½ cup white sugar
- 2 eggs
- 1 teaspoon vanilla
- 2 cups flour
- 1 teaspoon baking soda
- ¼ teaspoon salt
- 2 cups chocolate chips

Photo courtesy of The Gray Boxwood,
www.thegrayboxwood.com

Cream shortening, margarine, and sugars. Beat in eggs, then vanilla. Add dry ingredients, which have been sifted together. Stir in chips. Drop by teaspoons onto greased cookie sheets. Bake at 350°F for 10–11 minutes.

Chocolate Mint Cookies

- ¾ cup butter
- 1½ cups brown sugar
- 1 12-ounce package chocolate chips
- 2 tablespoons water
- 2 eggs
- 2½ cups flour
- 1¼ teaspoons baking soda
- ½ teaspoon salt
- Andes mints

Melt butter, sugar, and water in a saucepan over low heat. Remove from heat and add chocolate chips. Stir until chips are completely melted. Put in mixing bowl; let stand for 10 minutes to cool. Add eggs 1 at a time. Combine flour, baking soda, and salt; add to chocolate mixture. Chill dough for 1 hour. Roll into balls. Place on cookie sheets lined with parchment paper. Bake at 350°F for 8–10 minutes. Remove from oven. Place half an Andes mint on top of each hot cookie; allow to melt, then swirl a bit.

Tip: For best results in baking, always bring eggs to room temperature before adding them to your recipe.

Photo courtesy of The Gray Boxwood,
www.thegrayboxwood.com

Date Pinwheels

- ½ cup butter
- ½ cup brown sugar
- ½ cup white sugar
- 1 egg
- ½ teaspoon vanilla
- 2 cups pastry flour
- ⅛ teaspoon salt
- ¼ teaspoon baking soda

Filling:

- 7–8 ounces dates, cut
- ⅓ cup water
- ¼ cup sugar
- ⅛ teaspoon salt
- 1 cup nuts
- Grated rind of 1 lemon or 1 tablespoon lemon juice (optional)

Cream butter. Add sugars, egg, and vanilla in order given. Sift flour, salt, and baking soda together and add to butter mixture. Chill until firm enough to roll. Simmer all filling ingredients (except nuts) 5 minutes, stirring often. Add nuts and cool. If desired, add grated rind from 1 lemon or 1 tablespoon lemon juice. Roll cookie dough to 9 x 12-inch rectangle. Spread with cooled filling. Roll up tightly and wrap in wax paper. Chill or freeze overnight for easier slicing. Slice ⅛-inch thick. Bake on greased cookie sheet at 350°F–375°F for 10 minutes. Store in airtight container. Rolls may be kept in freezer and sliced for baking as needed.

 Medicine and advice are two things more pleasant to give than to receive.

Delicious Cookies

- 1 cup butter
- 1 cup oil
- 1 cup white sugar
- 1 cup brown sugar
- 1 egg
- 2 teaspoons vanilla
- 1 teaspoon coconut flavoring
- ½ teaspoon butter flavoring
- 1 teaspoon salt
- 1 teaspoon baking soda
- 1 teaspoon cream of tartar
- 3½ cups flour
- 1 cup quick oatmeal
- 1 cup Rice Krispies cereal
- 1 cup flaked coconut
- 6 ounces chocolate chips

Beat butter, oil, and sugars until creamy. Add egg and flavorings. Combine flour, salt, baking soda, and cream of tartar. Gradually add to butter mixture. Stir in remaining ingredients. Drop from scoop of your preferred size. Bake at 350°F for 10 minutes.

Gingersnaps

Makes about 3 dozen cookies

- ¾ cup melted butter or ½ cup melted margarine
- 1 cup sugar
- 1 egg, beaten
- 3 tablespoons molasses
- About 2 cups flour
- 1½ teaspoons baking soda
- 1 teaspoon cinnamon
- ½ teaspoon cloves
- ½ teaspoon ginger
- Sugar to cover

Cream butter and sugar. Add egg and molasses. Sift together dry ingredients. Add to creamed mixture. Form into small balls and roll in sugar. Bake at 350°F for 10–12 minutes.

Molasses Krinkles

- 2½ cups sifted pastry flour
- 2 teaspoons baking soda
- ½ teaspoon salt
- 1–2 teaspoons ginger to taste
- 1–2 teaspoons cinnamon to taste
- ¾ cup shortening
- 1 cup white sugar
- 1 egg, unbeaten
- 4 tablespoons molasses
- 1½ cups raisins *(optional)*
- Sugar to cover

Photo courtesy of The Gray Boxwood, www.thegrayboxwood.com

Sift flour once. Add baking soda and spices. Sift 3 times. Cream shortening. Add sugar and egg. Beat thoroughly. Add molasses, then add flour mixture gradually. Roll into 1¼-inch balls after dough is well chilled and roll in sugar. Bake on ungreased pan at 350°F for 15–20 minutes. To make Raisin Molasses Cookies, add 1 ½ cups raisins to this recipe.

Keep an open mind, but don't keep it too open, or people will throw a lot of rubbish into it.

Peanut Butter Chocolate Chip Cookies

- ¾ cup butter
- ½ cup peanut butter
- 1 cup white sugar
- 1 cup brown sugar
- 2 eggs
- 2 teaspoons vanilla
- 1 teaspoon baking soda
- ½ teaspoon salt
- 2½ cups flour
- 1 package chocolate chips

Beat butters and sugars until creamy. Add eggs and vanilla; beat well. Stir together baking soda, salt, and flour; gradually add to butter mixture, beating until well blended. Stir in chocolate chips. Drop by scoops of desired size onto baking sheet. Bake at 350°F for 10 minutes.

Peppernuts

- 2 cups (4 sticks) margarine
- 8 cups brown sugar
- 8 eggs
- 2 teaspoons anise oil
- 2 teaspoons baking soda dissolved in ¼ cup hot water
- 9 cups flour, divided
- 2 teaspoons cream of tartar
- 2 teaspoons cinnamon
- 2 teaspoons nutmeg
- 2 teaspoons ground cloves

Cream margarine and sugar in a large bowl. Add eggs and anise oil. Mix well. Add dissolved baking soda. Mix together 4 cups of the flour with the cream of tartar, cinnamon, nutmeg, and cloves. Add to the creamed mixture. Gradually add remaining flour. Roll into long, thin rolls and freeze. To bake, cut frozen rolls into thin slices. Place on greased cookie sheets. Bake at 350°F for 8–10 minutes.

Photo courtesy of The Gray Boxwood, www.thegrayboxwood.com

Rich Sugar Cookies

- 1 cup butter
- 1 cup white sugar
- 1 cup powdered sugar
- 1 cup oil
- 2 eggs, beaten
- 2 teaspoons vanilla
- 1 teaspoon cream of tartar
- 1 teaspoon baking soda
- 5¼ cups flour

Powdered icing:
- 1 cup powdered sugar
- ½ teaspoon vanilla
- 1–2 tablespoons milk
- Food coloring *(optional)*

Blend sugars, butter, and oil well; add beaten eggs and vanilla. Mix dry ingredients together and add to egg mixture. Drop onto cookie sheets with your favorite size of cookie scoop; flatten with a fork. Bake at 350°F for 10 minutes.

For icing, mix powdered sugar, vanilla, milk (1 tablespoon at a time), and food coloring until spreadable (mixture will thicken slightly as it sets).

Sorghum Cookies

- 1 cup sugar
- ¾ cup shortening
- 1 egg
- 4 tablespoons sorghum syrup
- 1 teaspoon cinnamon
- ¼ teaspoon salt
- 2 teaspoons powdered ginger
- 2 scant teaspoons baking soda
- 2 cups flour
- Sugar to cover

Beat sugar, shortening, egg, and sorghum syrup until creamy. Combine dry ingredients and add to shortening mixture; mix well. Chill for 2 hours. To form the cookies, make 1¼-inch balls. Roll each ball in sugar. Place the cookies on the prepared baking sheet about 1–2 inches apart, and bake for 6–7 minutes. (It's important not to overbake the cookies; make sure they stay soft and gooey.) Cool on a rack.

Applesauce Bars

- 1 cup shortening
- 1½ cups sugar
- 2 eggs
- 2½ cups flour
- 1 cup unsweetened applesauce
- ½ cup raisins
- 1 teaspoon baking soda
- ½ teaspoon salt
- 1 teaspoon cinnamon
- ¼ teaspoon cloves
- ½ cup chopped nuts
- Powdered sugar

Cream shortening and sugar and beat in eggs one at a time. Blend thoroughly. Combined dry ingredients; add flour alternately with applesauce. Add nuts and raisins. Spread in a greased 10 x 15-inch pan or two 8 x 8-inch pans. Bake at 350°F for 30 minutes. Dust with powdered sugar.

Tip: These bars are more moist and even more delicious if they are made a day ahead of serving.

Lemon Squares

- 1 cup white sugar
- 2 tablespoons cornstarch, rounded
- 2 eggs, slightly beaten
- 1 cup cold water
- ¼ cup butter, melted
- ½ teaspoon vanilla
- Juice and rind of 1 lemon

Crumbs:
- 1 cup saltine cracker crumbs
- ½ cup butter
- 1 cup brown sugar
- 1 cup coconut
- ½ teaspoon baking soda
- 1 cup flour

Combine ingredients to make crumbs. Press three-fourths of crumbs in bottom of 9 x 9-inch pan. Bake 25 minutes at 325°F. Combine filling ingredients and spread over baked crumbs. Sprinkle with remaining crumbs. Bake 20 minutes longer.

Rice Krispie Roll Ups

- 1 10-ounce bag marshmallows
- ¼ cup butter
- ¼ cup peanut butter
- 5½ cups Rice Krispies cereal
- 1 cup chocolate chips
- ¾ cup butterscotch chips

Line a 10 x 15-inch pan with parchment paper and set aside. In a microwave-safe bowl, combine the marshmallows, butter, and peanut butter. Cover and microwave on high for 1½ minutes; stir until well blended. Put Rice Krispies in a large bowl and pour butter mixture over top; stir until cereal is well coated. Spread onto prepared pan.

In a microwave-safe bowl, combine chocolate and butterscotch chips. Microwave, uncovered, on high for 1½ minutes. Stir; spread over cereal mixture to within 1 inch of edges. Roll up jelly roll-style, starting with a short side, peeling parchment paper away while rolling. Place, seam side down, on a serving plate. Refrigerate for 1 hour or until set. Cut into ½-inch slices. Store in refrigerator or freezer.

Tip: Do not mistake these for simple children's Rice Krispies treats. They are irresistible for people of all ages. Your family will request them again and again, and your friends will be asking you for the recipe.

" *Kindness, when given away, keeps coming back.* "

Rocky Road Bars

- 1 cup butter
- 1½ cups sugar
- 4 eggs
- 2 teaspoons vanilla
- ½ teaspoon salt
- ½ teaspoon baking powder
- ¼ cup cocoa
- 1½ cups flour
- 4 cups miniature marshmallows

Topping:

- 1½ cups milk chocolate chips
- 1½ cups peanut butter (can use less if preferred)
- 2¼ cups Rice Krispies cereal

Beat butter and sugar until creamy. Add eggs and vanilla. Gradually add dry ingredients. Put in 10 x 15-inch greased pan. Bake at 350°F for 15 minutes. Remove from oven. Sprinkle miniature marshmallows on top and put back in oven; bake until marshmallows are puffy. Cool well before adding the topping.

For the topping, melt chocolate chips and peanut butter together in microwave. Stir in Rice Krispies. Spread over marshmallows. Cool well before cutting.

Blonde Brownies

- 2 cups brown sugar
- ⅔ cup butter, softened at room temperature
- 2 eggs
- 1 teaspoon vanilla
- 2 cups flour
- 1 teaspoon baking powder
- ¼ teaspoon baking soda
- Pinch of salt
- ¾ cup flaked coconut
- 1 cup chocolate chips

Beat together brown sugar, butter, eggs, and vanilla until creamy. Combine flour, baking powder, baking soda, and salt. Beat into butter mixture. Stir in coconut and chocolate chips; it is a very stiff dough. Spoon onto a 10 x 15-inch cookie sheet with sides. Spread to 1 inch from the edges of the pan. Bake at 325°F for 30–35 minutes until golden brown; do not overbake. Cool for a few minutes in the pan and then cut into squares. Remove from pan after cooled completely.

Tip: These are a delicious, soft, and chewy alternative to chocolate chip cookies.

Buttermilk Brownies

- 1 cup butter
- 3 tablespoons cocoa powder
- 1 cup water
- 2 cups sugar
- 2 eggs, beaten
- ½ teaspoon salt
- 1 teaspoon baking soda
- 1 teaspoon vanilla
- 2 cups flour
- ½ cup buttermilk

Frosting:

- ¼ cup butter
- 3 tablespoons cocoa powder
- 3 tablespoons buttermilk
- 2¼ cups powdered sugar
- 1 teaspoon vanilla

In a saucepan, combine butter, cocoa, water, and sugar. Bring to boil, stirring constantly. Remove from heat and set aside. In a large bowl, mix together flour, baking soda, and salt. In a small bowl, combine buttermilk, eggs, and vanilla; whisk lightly with a fork. Pour the buttermilk mixture into dry ingredients; mix until smooth.

Add cocoa mixture gradually with mixer on low setting. Mix until well blended, scraping down the sides. Pour into greased 10 x 15-inch pan. Bake at 350°F for 20–25 minutes or until toothpick inserted in the center comes out clean.

For frosting, melt butter, cocoa, and buttermilk in a saucepan. Stir in the sugar and vanilla. Spread over warm brownies before cutting. Be careful not to crumble the brownies, as they are tender.

Jumping for joy is good exercise.

Butterscotch Brownies

- ¼ cup butter or butter-flavored vegetable shortening
- 1 cup packed light brown sugar
- 1 egg
- ¾ cup flour
- 1 teaspoon baking powder
- ½ teaspoon salt
- ½ teaspoon vanilla
- ½ cup chopped nuts

Preheat oven to 350°F. Melt butter over low heat. Remove from heat and blend in sugar. Cool and stir in egg. Blend in flour, baking powder, and salt. Mix in vanilla and nuts. Spread in a well-greased 8-inch square pan. Bake 25 minutes. Cut into bars while still warm.

Cake Flour Brownies

- ½ cup butter
- 1 cup sugar
- 2 eggs
- 2 squares baking chocolate, melted
- 1 cup cake flour, sifted
- ½ teaspoon baking powder
- ½ teaspoon salt
- ½ cup nutmeats
- ½ teaspoon vanilla

Cream butter with sugar. Add eggs one at a time, beating well after each addition. Add cooled melted chocolate. Sift dry ingredients together and add to creamed mixture. Add nutmeats and vanilla. Bake at 350°F for 25–30 minutes. Cool and cut into bars to serve.

Speedy Brownies

- 2 cups brown sugar
- 1¾ cups all-purpose flour
- ½ teaspoon salt
- 5 eggs
- 1 cup vegetable oil
- 1 teaspoon vanilla
- 1 cup chocolate chips
- Powdered sugar

Mix the first 6 ingredients. Beat well and pour into a cake pan. Sprinkle with chocolate chips and powdered sugar. Bake at 350°F for 30 minutes.

Ice Water Pie Pastry

Makes 3 piecrusts
- 2½ cups pastry flour
- 1 teaspoon salt
- ½ teaspoon baking powder
- ¾ cup corn oil
- 1 tablespoon vinegar
- Ice water

Sift together the pastry flour, salt, and baking powder. Measure the corn oil into a cup. Add the vinegar and fill with ice water to measure 1 cup total. Add to dry ingredients and blend all with a fork. Roll on wax paper.

Tip: If you want a tender and flaky piecrust, don't over-flour the pastry crust as you roll it out.

No Fail Piecrust

Makes 3 piecrusts
- 3 cups flour
- 1 teaspoon salt
- 1 cup shortening
- ¼ cup water
- ¼ cup oil
- ¼ cup milk

Mix flour and salt together; cut in the shortening with a pastry cutter. Add liquids and mix.

 Quick and Easy!

Photo courtesy of The Gray Boxwood, www.thegrayboxwood.com

Apple Cream Pie

- 1 9-inch piecrust, unbaked
- 3 cups thinly sliced apples, preferably Yellow Delicious
- 1 cup plus 1 tablespoon sugar, divided
- ¼ cup flour
- ⅛ teaspoon salt
- ¾ cup heavy cream
- 1 teaspoon cinnamon

Combine 1 cup sugar, flour, salt, and cream and beat until thick. Add to sliced apples and put into piecrust. Combine 1 tablespoon sugar and 1 teaspoon cinnamon; sprinkle over apples. Bake at 400°F for 10 minutes and then at 350°F for 40–45 minutes.

Apple Crumb Pie

- 4–6 tart apples
- 1 cup sugar, divided
- ⅓ cup butter
- ¾ cup flour
- 1 teaspoon cinnamon
- 1 9-inch piecrust, unbaked

Peel apples; cut into eighths. Mix ½ cup sugar and cinnamon together. Sprinkle over the apples. Put apple mixture in unbaked piecrust. Combine ½ cup sugar with the flour; add to butter. Crumble mixture with a pastry cutter. Sprinkle crumb mixture over apples. Bake at 400°F for 10 minutes. Reduce heat to 350°. Bake for 35 minutes longer or until apples are tender. Serve with a scoop of vanilla ice cream.

Tip: To prevent a piecrust from becoming too brown, place a shield of aluminum foil over the edge of the pastry crust when it's baking; remove this shield for the last 15 minutes of baking time.

Dutch Apple Pie

- Apples, sliced into wedges
- ½ cup sour cream, ¼ cup milk, or ¼ cup water
- 2 tablespoons lemon juice
- Butter
- 1 piecrust, unbaked

Crumbs:
- 1 cup brown sugar
- ⅓ cup flour
- ½ teaspoon cinnamon

Mix the ingredients for the crumbs. Spread ⅓ of the mixture over the bottom of the piecrust. Cover this with layers of the apple wedges. The top layer may be arranged in a design, such as sixths in a circle. Cover with the remaining crumbs. Spoon the sour cream, milk, or water and the lemon juice over the apples. If milk or water are used, dot with butter for additional glaze. Bake at 450°F for 10 minutes, then at 375°F for 40 minutes.

Big Valley Half Moon Pies

Mix dry ingredients for piecrust. In a cup, beat the egg and vinegar. Fill the cup half full with cold water and add to dry ingredients. To make the filling, cook the apples until soft with as little water as possible, then mash. Add remaining ingredients.

Form pie dough into balls the size of a large walnut. Roll each ball into a round, flat shape. On one half, make several holes with a pie crimper. On the other half, add a heaping tablespoon of cooled apple filling. Fold the half with holes over the filled side. Press edges together firmly and trim around the edges with a pie crimper. Bake at 375°F for 20 minutes.

Piecrust:
- 1 cup shortening
- 2½ cups flour
- ½ teaspoon baking powder
- 1 teaspoon salt
- 1 egg
- 1 teaspoon vinegar
- Cold water

Filling:
- 6 cups cooked snitz (dried apples)
- 2 cups brown sugar
- 1 cup white sugar
- 4 teaspoons cinnamon
- ½ cup flour
- 3 teaspoons lemon juice
- ¼ teaspoon salt

Buttermilk Pie

- 1 cup sugar
- 2 tablespoons flour
- ½ teaspoon baking soda
- 2 tablespoons butter, melted
- 2 eggs
- 1 teaspoon lemon juice
- 2 cups buttermilk
- 1 10-inch pie shell, unbaked

Combine the sugar, flour, and baking soda. Beat the melted butter, eggs, and lemon juice. Add the sugar mixture and buttermilk. Pour into unbaked 10-inch pie shell. Bake at 425°F for 10 minutes and at 350°F for 35 minutes.

Coconut Pie

- 1 envelope unflavored gelatin
- ¼ cup sugar
- ⅛ teaspoon salt
- 3 eggs, separated
- 1¾ cups milk
- 1 teaspoon vanilla
- ¾ cup flaked coconut
- ¼ cup sugar
- 1 9-inch pie shell, baked
- Maraschino cherries or fresh fruit for topping (optional)

Mix the gelatin, ¼ cup sugar, and salt in top of double boiler. Beat together the egg yolks and milk. Add to gelatin mixture. Cook, stirring constantly, until gelatin dissolves. Remove from heat and stir in vanilla. Chill, stirring occasionally, until mixture mounds. Stir in the coconut. Make a meringue of the egg whites and ¼ cup sugar. Fold into gelatin mixture and pile in baked 9-inch pie shell. Chill. Top can be garnished with maraschino cherries or fresh fruits in season.

Custard Pie

- 4 eggs
- ½ cup sugar
- ¼ teaspoon salt
- 2½ cups milk
- ½ teaspoon vanilla
- Pinch nutmeg
- 1 pie shell, unbaked

Beat eggs slightly. Mix in sugar, salt, milk, vanilla, and nutmeg. Pour into unbaked pie shell. Bake at 400°F for 25–30 minutes.

Elderberry Pie

- 1 cup applesauce
- 1 pie shell, unbaked
- 1½ cups elderberries
- 1 cup sugar

Spread applesauce over the bottom of the unbaked pie shell, and then add the elderberries and sugar. Bake at 425°F for 10 minutes or 375°F for 30 minutes.

Living the Simple Life

Traditionally the Amish derive essentially all of their household income from their own business-related activities. The Amish value rural life, and many families own and operate small farms. Some have opened small shops and earn money selling their handmade wares such as quilts and furniture directly to consumers.

Grape Pie

- 5 cups Concord grapes
- 1 egg
- 1 cup sugar
- 2 tablespoons flour
- 1 tablespoon butter
- 1 tablespoon lemon juice
- 1 pie shell, unbaked

Crumbs:
- ¼ cup flour
- ¼ cup sugar
- 2 tablespoons butter

Topping:
- 1 egg white, beaten
- 2 tablespoons sugar

Wash the grapes and squeeze the pulp from the skins. Cook pulp 5 minutes and press through a sieve to separate the seeds. Beat the egg. Add the sugar, flour, butter, and lemon juice. Add the skins and the pulp. Pour into unbaked pie shell and cover with a lattice top of pastry strips or top with crumbs, made by combining the listed ingredients. Bake at 400° for 45 minutes. Combine ingredients for topping and serve with pie.

Grasshopper Pie

- 24 cream-filled chocolate cookies, crushed
- ¼ cup margarine, melted
- ¼ cup milk
- Few drops peppermint extract
- Few drops green food coloring
- 1 jar marshmallow créme
- 2 cups heavy cream, whipped

Combine crushed cookies and margarine. Press into 9-inch spring pan, reserving ½ cup of mixture for topping. Gradually add milk, peppermint extract, and food coloring to marshmallow créme. Mix until well blended. Fold in whipped cream. Pour into pan and sprinkle with remaining crumbs. Freeze. Remove 30 minutes before serving.

Household Hint

Clean your coffee percolator by perking baking soda in water. Rinse thoroughly.

Lemon Sponge Pie

- 2 egg yolks
- Grated rind and juice of 1 lemon
- 1 cup sugar
- 3 tablespoons flour
- 3 tablespoons butter
- ¼ teaspoon salt
- 1 cup milk
- 2 beaten egg whites
- 1 pie shell, unbaked

Preheat oven to 425°F. Beat all the ingredients, except the egg whites, together in order given. Then add the egg whites. Pour into unbaked pie shell. Put pie in and reduce to 250°F for 40 minutes.

 Use it up, wear it out, make it do, or do without.

Montgomery County or Lemon Drop Pie

Makes 2 9-inch pies

Top Portion:

- 2½ cups flour
- ½ cup butter or lard
- 3 teaspoons baking powder
- 2 eggs, beaten
- 2 cups sugar
- 1 cup whole milk

Bottom Portion:

- 1 egg, beaten
- 2 teaspoons flour
- Juice and grated rind of 1 large lemon
- 1 cup sugar
- 1 cup molasses
- 2 9-inch pie shells, unbaked

For the top portion, sift together flour and baking powder. Combine butter, sugar, and cream thoroughly. Mix in well-beaten eggs; add milk and sifted dry ingredients alternately. Set aside while you make the bottom portion.

For the bottom portion, combine all ingredients. Pour into 2 unbaked pie shells. Spoon top portion over this mixture. Bake at 350°F for 35–40 minutes.

Mincemeat

- 1½ pounds beef
- 1½ pounds pork
- ½ pound suet
- 2 pounds seedless raisins
- 2 pounds currants
- 2 pounds granulated sugar
- 1 pound brown sugar
- 2 oranges
- 2 lemons
- ½ pound citron peel
- 2 quarts peeled and cored apples
- 1 cup molasses
- 2 teaspoons ground cloves
- 3 teaspoons cinnamon
- 3 teaspoons nutmeg
- 1 cup cider

Cook beef, pork, and suet until tender. Mince fine or put through chopper. Put the apples, oranges, and lemons through chopper. Mix all ingredients thoroughly. Bring to a boil and simmer 12 minutes. Put in jars and seal while hot.

Glazed Peach Pie

- 4 cups fresh, sliced peaches
- 1 cup sugar
- 3 tablespoons cornstarch
- ½ cup water
- 1 tablespoon butter
- Almond flavoring
- 1 9-inch piecrust, baked
- Whipped cream or ice cream

Crush enough of the peaches to make 1 cup of crushed peaches. Put remaining sliced peaches in baked pie shell. Whisk together the sugar and cornstarch. Combine the crushed peaches with the sugar cornstarch mixture and add water. Put in heavy saucepan and cook until mixture is clear. Remove from heat; add butter and almond flavoring. Pour into glass bowl and cool slightly. Pour over sliced peaches in piecrust and refrigerate for at least 2 hours. Top with whipped cream or ice cream.

 If the grass looks greener on the other side, fertilize.

Peach Cobbler

Bottom Layer:
- 5 cups sliced peaches
- ¾ cup sugar
- 2 tablespoons flour
- ½ teaspoon cinnamon
- ¼ teaspoon salt
- 1 teaspoon vanilla
- 1 tablespoon butter

Upper Layer:
- 1 cup flour
- 1 cup sugar
- 1 teaspoon baking powder
- ½ teaspoon salt
- 4 tablespoons butter
- 2 eggs, slightly beaten

Mix ingredients for bottom layer together and pour into a 9 x 13-inch pan. Mix together ingredients for upper layer and pour over ingredients in pan. Bake at 350°F for 30–35 minutes.

Peanut Butter Pie

Combine egg yolks, milk, sugar, peanut butter, flour, and salt. Cook until thickened, stirring often. Cool slightly. Pour into baked pie shell. Top with your favorite meringue. Place in a hot oven just long enough to brown meringue.

- 2 egg yolks
- 1½ cups scalded milk
- 1 cup brown sugar
- 3 tablespoons peanut butter
- 1 tablespoon flour or 1½ teaspoons cornstarch
- ¼ teaspoon salt
- 1 pie shell, baked
- Meringue

Pink Lady Pie

- 1 9-inch piecrust, baked
- 2 cups fresh, diced rhubarb
- 1 cup sugar
- 1 3-ounce package strawberry gelatin
- 1 tablespoon lemon juice
- 2 cups whipped cream or whipped topping

Cook rhubarb and sugar slowly until tender. Add dry gelatin. Stir gently until dissolved; let cool. Add lemon juice; cool to room temperature. Fold rhubarb mixture into baked crust. Refrigerate. Top with whipped cream or whipped topping when serving.

Pumpkin Pie

- 1½ cups cooked pumpkin
- 1 teaspoon flour
- 1 cup sugar
- 1 teaspoon cinnamon
- 1 teaspoon ginger
- ⅛ teaspoon nutmeg
- ½ teaspoon mace
- ¼ teaspoon salt
- 3 eggs, well beaten
- ½ cup milk
- Pastry for deep-dish single-crust pie

Mix pumpkin, flour, sugar, spices, and salt. Combine beaten eggs and milk. Add to pumpkin mixture. Stir it all together. Pour into a deep pie plate lined with a good, rich pastry. Bake at 350°F for about 35 minutes.

Photo courtesy of The Gray Boxwood, www.thegrayboxwood.com

Dry-Bottom Shoofly Pie

Photo courtesy of Discover Lancaster

- 1 cup flour
- ¾ cup brown sugar
- 1 rounded tablespoon shortening
- 1 cup molasses
- 1 egg, beaten
- ¾ cup hot water
- 1 teaspoon baking soda
- 1 9-inch piecrust, unbaked

Mix flour, brown sugar, and shortening with a pastry blender. Reserve ⅔ cup for topping. Spoon the rest into the unbaked piecrust. Mix baking soda in hot water. Add egg and molasses. Stir and pour into dry mixture in piecrust. Sprinkle reserved crumbs on top. Bake at 400°F for 10 minutes, then at 350°F for 30 minutes.

 Household Hint:

If you run out of filters for your drip pot or percolator, simply cut a paper towel to size.

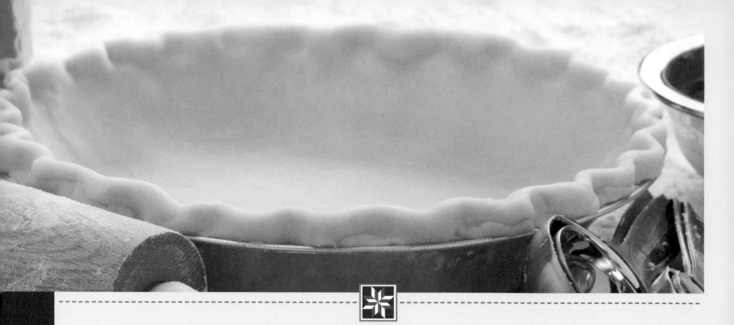

Wet-Bottom Shoofly Pie

- 1½ cups all-purpose flour
- ½ cup brown sugar
- 2 tablespoons shortening
- 1 teaspoon baking soda
- 1 cup boiling water
- ½ cup dark corn syrup
- ½ cup molasses
- ¼ teaspoon salt
- 1 egg
- 1 9-inch piecrust, unbaked

Preheat oven to 375°F. Combine flour, brown sugar, and shortening. Cut ingredients together with a pastry cutter until dough forms fine crumbs. Set aside.

Dissolve the baking soda in the boiling water. Stir in corn syrup, molasses, salt, and egg, being sure to stir well. Pour ⅓ of mixture into unbaked piecrust. Sprinkle ⅓ of the crumbs over mixture. Continue this process until crumb mixture and liquid mixture have been used up.

Bake in preheated oven for 10 minutes, then lower oven temperature to 350°F and bake for an additional 30 minutes.

Sour Cream Raisin Pie

- 2 eggs, beaten
- ¾ cup sugar
- 1 cup sour cream
- ¼ teaspoon salt
- 1 teaspoon cinnamon
- ¼ teaspoon cloves
- 1 cup raisins, uncooked
- 1 9-inch piecrust, unbaked

Combine ingredients and put into piecrust. Bake at 400°F for 20–25 minutes or until center is set.

Household Hint

To clean brass, rub ketchup on a soft cloth and polish. Rinse.

Strawberry Pie

- 1 quart strawberries
- ½ cup water
- 3 tablespoons cornstarch
- 1 cup sugar
- 1 tablespoon butter
- 1 tablespoon lemon juice
- Few grains salt
- 1 pie shell, baked
- Whipped cream

Sort the strawberries into 2 equal parts. Crush the part that has the imperfect berries. Cut the remaining berries into quarters or halves depending on size. Add the water mixed with the cornstarch to the crushed berries. Cook until thick and clear. Add the sugar, butter, lemon juice, and a few grains salt. Cool. Add reserved cut berries. Pour into baked shell. Chill. Serve with whipped cream.

Vanilla Pie

- 2 cups brown sugar
- 5 tablespoons flour
- 1 cup maple syrup
- 4 cups hot water
- 2 teaspoons vanilla
- 3 pie shells, unbaked

Crumbs:
- 2 cups flour
- 1 cup brown sugar
- 1 teaspoon baking soda
- 1 teaspoon cream of tartar
- 1 cup butter

To make the filling, mix the brown sugar and the flour. Add the maple syrup and hot water. Cook until starch is cooked and is syrupy. Cool and add the vanilla. Make the crumb mixture by using fingertips to blend the flour, brown sugar, baking soda, cream of tartar, and butter. Divide the filling into 3 unbaked pie shells. Divide the crumbs and sprinkle over the 3 pies. Bake at 425°F for 10 minutes and then reduce to 325°F for 25 minutes.

Tip: Strawberries will stay firm for several days if they are stored in a colander in the refrigerator. The colander allows cold air to circulate through and around them, keeping them fresh.

Angel Food Cake

- 2 cups egg whites (1 dozen jumbo eggs)
- 2 teaspoons cream of tartar
- ½ teaspoon salt
- 2 cups sugar
- 2 cups cake flour sifted with ½ cup sugar
- 2 teaspoons vanilla

Sauce:

- ½ cup white sugar
- 2 tablespoons cornstarch
- 1 egg
- 1 cup pineapple juice or diluted lemon juice
- 1 envelope prepared whipped topping mix

Beat egg whites until foamy. Add cream of tartar and beat just until stiff enough to stand in peaks. Add salt. Slowly add the 2 cups sugar, continuing to beat until stiff peaks form. Fold in flour-sugar mixture and, finally, vanilla.

Put in tube pan and into cold oven. Turn heat to 350°F for 20 minutes, then to 350°F–375°F for 10–15 minutes. Invert cake to cool. Cook first 4 sauce ingredients over low heat until mixture thickens. Remove from heat and cool. Mix with whipped topping.

Dried Apple Cake

- 2 cups dried apples
- 2 cups molasses
- 1 cup butter
- 2 cups brown sugar
- 1 cup sour milk
- 2 eggs
- 2 teaspoons baking soda
- 4 cups flour
- Spices as desired

Soak the apples in water overnight. Drain and simmer for 1 hour with the molasses. Add the butter and cool. Add the brown sugar, milk, eggs, baking soda, flour, and desired spices (such as cinnamon or cloves). Bake in loaf pans.

Banana Cake

- ⅔ cup soft shortening
- 2½ cups cake flour
- 1⅔ cups sugar
- 1¼ teaspoons baking powder
- 1 teaspoon baking soda
- 1 teaspoon salt
- 1¼ cups mashed bananas
- ⅓ cup buttermilk
- 2 eggs

Measure shortening into a large mixing bowl. Sift flour, sugar, baking powder, baking soda, and salt. Add to shortening. Add mashed bananas. Use beater to blend all, then beat 2 minutes on medium speed. Add buttermilk and eggs. Beat 2 minutes longer. Bake at 350°F in 2 9-inch layer pans or a 9 x 13-inch pan.

Tip: Fruits, nuts, and raisins often sink to the bottom of cake batter. To keep them evenly dispersed, try heating them or rolling them in melted butter before adding them to the batter.

Carrot Cake

- 4 eggs
- 2 cups sugar
- 1½ cups oil
- 1 teaspoon vanilla
- 3 cups shredded carrots
- 2 cups flour
- 2 teaspoons baking soda
- 1 teaspoon baking powder
- 1½ teaspoons cinnamon
- 1 teaspoon salt
- 1 cup chopped walnuts
  or pecans *(optional)*

Cream cheese icing:
- ½ cup butter
- 3 ounces cream cheese
- 2 teaspoons vanilla
- 2 cups powdered sugar
  or more as needed for consistency

Beat eggs well. Add sugar; beat until creamy. Beat in oil and vanilla. Stir in carrots. Combine flour, baking soda, baking powder, cinnamon, and salt. Add dry ingredients to egg/sugar mixture. Stir in nuts. Pour into ungreased 9 x 13-inch pan and bake at 350°F for 40–45 minutes or until toothpick inserted in center comes out clean. Cool completely. Spread with cream cheese icing. Keep cake refrigerated.

Down-Side-Up Fudge Cake

- 1 tablespoon solid vegetable shortening
- ¾ cup white sugar
- ½ cup milk
- 1 teaspoon vanilla
- 1 cup flour
- 1½ tablespoons cocoa
- 1 teaspoon baking powder
- ½ teaspoon salt

Topping:
- ½ cup chopped nuts *(optional)*
- ¼ cup cocoa
- ½ cup white sugar
- ½ cup brown sugar
- 1¼ cups boiling water

To make the cake batter, cream shortening and sugar. Stir in milk and vanilla. Sift together flour, cocoa, baking powder, and salt. Add to creamed mixture, mixing thoroughly. Pour into greased 8-inch square pan. Top batter with nuts. Combine cocoa and sugars and sprinkle evenly over nuts. Pour the boiling water (be sure it's boiling) over batter and topping. Bake at 350°F for 35 minutes. Cool 15 minutes, then invert cake onto serving plate. Serve plain or with whipped topping. You can decrease the amount of cocoa, if desired, and omit the nuts.

Photo courtesy of The Gray Boxwood,
www.thegrayboxwood.com

Tip: Before you put a cake on a plate, sprinkle sugar on the plate to absorb moisture. Otherwise, the bottom of the cake may get gooey and stick to the plate.

174

Fruit Cocktail Cake

- 2 large eggs
- 1½ cups white sugar
- 2 cups unsifted all-purpose flour
- 2 teaspoons baking soda
- 1 14-ounce can fruit cocktail

Topping:
- ½ cup butter
- 1 cup white sugar
- ½ cup evaporated milk
- 1 cup coconut
- 1 teaspoon vanilla
- ¾ cup chopped nuts

To prepare batter, beat eggs and sugar. Sift together flour and baking soda. Add dry ingredients to first mixture alternately with fruit cocktail (include syrup). Bake at 350°F in 9 x 13-inch pan. To prepare topping, mix all ingredients in a small saucepan. Boil together 2 minutes and spread on warm cake.

Jelly Roll

Beat egg whites until very stiff. Add sugar. Beat egg yolks and mix into beaten whites. Add flour, baking powder, and vanilla. Mix well. Line a rimmed cookie sheet with waxed paper or spray with cooking spray. Spread batter over sheet. Bake at 325°F–350°F for 10–15 minutes. Remove from cookie sheet immediately after baking and place on counter, which has been spread with sugar. (This coats the outside of the jelly roll with sugar.) Spread pie filling or jam on cake. Roll up.

- 6 eggs, separated
- 1 cup sugar
- 1 cup white flour
- 1 teaspoon baking powder
- 1 teaspoon vanilla
- 1 can lemon pie filling or jar strawberry jam
- Sugar to cover

Simple and Delicious

Lazy Daisy Oatmeal Cake

- 1¼ cups boiling water
- 1 cup oatmeal
- ½ cup shortening
- 1 cup white sugar
- 1 cup brown sugar, packed
- 1 teaspoon vanilla
- 2 eggs
- 1½ cups sifted flour
- 1 teaspoon baking soda
- ½ teaspoon salt
- ¾ teaspoon cinnamon
- ¼ teaspoon nutmeg

Frosting:

- ¼ cup butter, melted
- ½ cup brown sugar
- 3 tablespoons cream
- ⅓ cup chopped nutmeats
- ¾ cup coconut

Pour water over oatmeal. Cover and let stand 20 minutes. Beat shortening until creamy. Gradually add sugars and beat until fluffy. Blend in vanilla and eggs. Add oatmeal. Mix well. Sift together dry ingredients and add to creamed mixture. Mix well. Pour into greased and floured 9-inch pan. Bake at 350°F for 50 minutes. Combine all frosting ingredients and spread over warm cake. Broil until frosting becomes bubbly and lightly browned.

 Tip: When testing to see if a cake is done, you can use a stick of uncooked spaghetti if you're out of toothpicks.

Pumpkin Roll

- 3 eggs
- ⅔ cup cooked pumpkin
- 1 teaspoon baking powder
- ¾ cup flour
- 1 cup sugar
- 1 teaspoon salt
- ½ teaspoon cinnamon

Filling:

- 1 8-ounce package cream cheese, softened
- 2 tablespoons butter, softened
- 1 teaspoon vanilla
- 1 cup powdered sugar

Mix all cake ingredients in a bowl with a spoon. Grease a jelly roll pan and line with waxed paper. Spread batter over bottom of pan. Bake at 375°F for 15 minutes. Sprinkle powdered sugar on a clean tea towel. Turn pan over on tea towel to remove cake. Roll up as for jelly roll. Let cool. While cake is cooling, prepare filling by beating all ingredients until smooth. Unroll cooled cake and spread filling over the inside. Roll back up. Refrigerate until serving time.

Red Velvet Cake

- 2 eggs
- 1½ cups sugar
- ½ cup shortening
- 2 tablespoons cocoa powder
- 1 teaspoon baking soda
- 1 teaspoon salt
- 1 tablespoon vinegar
- 1 teaspoon vanilla
- 1½ tablespoons red food coloring
- 2½ cups flour
- 1 cup buttermilk

Vanilla cream cheese frosting:
- 1 8-ounce package cream cheese, softened
- ¼ cup butter, softened
- 2 tablespoons sour cream
- 2 teaspoons vanilla
- 1 16-ounce box powdered sugar

Grease and flour two 8- or 9-inch round cake pans. Cream butter and sugar in mixer bowl until fluffy. Add eggs and beat well. Place cocoa and food coloring in small bowl and stir to a smooth consistency. Add to creamed mixture. Sift flour and salt. Add flour mixture alternately with buttermilk, beating in between each addition. Add vanilla, vinegar, and baking soda. Mix well. Pour evenly into prepared cake pans and bake at 350°F for about 25 minutes.

Remove from oven and let cake rest for about 5 minutes, then remove from pans. Cool completely and then, with a large serrated knife, slice each cake horizontally, making a total of four layers. Wrap each cooled layer in plastic wrap and store in freezer overnight. Freezing the cake keeps the crumbs to a minimum when you are frosting it. Remove from freezer and frost immediately.

Sauerkraut Cake

- 2¼ cups all-purpose flour
- ½ cup cocoa
- 1 teaspoon baking powder
- 1 teaspoon baking soda
- ¼ teaspoon salt
- ⅔ cup sauerkraut (drained and rinsed)
- ⅔ cup butter
- 1½ cups sugar
- 3 large eggs
- 1 teaspoon vanilla
- 1 cup strong, cooled coffee or water

Combine first 5 ingredients. Cream butter and sugar. Add in 1 egg at a time. Add vanilla, coffee or water, and flour mixture alternately, beginning and ending with flour mixture. Stir in sauerkraut and bake at 350°F for 20–25 minutes in a 9 x 13-inch pan or layer cake pans.

Shoofly Cake

- 4 cups flour
- 2⅔ cups sugar
- 1 cup shortening
- 2 teaspoons baking soda
- 2 cups hot water
- 1 cup molasses

Preheat oven to 350°F. Combine flour, sugar, and shortening to make crumbs; reserve 1 cup. Dissolve baking soda in water; stir in molasses. Combine mixture with crumbs. Pour batter into greased 13 x 9-inch pan. Sprinkle with reserved crumbs. Bake for 30–40 minutes or until a toothpick comes out clean.

Wacky Cake

- 3 cups flour
- 2 cups sugar
- ½ cup cocoa
- 2 teaspoons baking soda
- 1 teaspoon salt
- 2 tablespoons vinegar
- 2 teaspoons vanilla
- ⅔ cup salad oil
- 2 cups water

Sift the first 5 ingredients into an ungreased 9 x 12-inch pan. Mix and make three holes. Pour vinegar, vanilla, and salad oil into holes. Pour water over top and mix until all ingredients are blended. Bake at 350°F for 30–35 minutes.

Living the Simple Life

The Amish wear simple, plain clothes, and they never wear any jewelry. Their clothes are homemade. They don't own a pair of shoes to go with every outfit. They see ever-changing fashion as wasteful and vain. Buying fewer clothes and unnecessary material things is one way to simplify your living. We can often get by on much less than we think.

Icing

- 1 cup milk
- 5 tablespoons flour
- ½–1 cup shortening
- 1 cup sugar
- Salt to taste
- Vanilla to taste

Mix milk and flour. Boil until very thick. Cool. Beat shortening. Add sugar and beat until fluffy. Add this slowly to cooked mixture. Beat for 15 minutes. Add salt and vanilla. This will keep in refrigerator for weeks and is ready to use any time.

Easy Chocolate Frosting

Bring all ingredients except chocolate chips to a full boil and boil for 30 seconds. Add chocolate chips. Stir until blended.

- 6 tablespoons butter
- ¼ cup plus 2 tablespoons milk
- 1½ cups sugar
- ⅓ cup chocolate chips

Maple Cream Icing

- 1 cup brown sugar
- 3 tablespoons milk
- 1 tablespoon butter
- Powdered sugar
- Vanilla or maple flavoring to taste

Mix sugar, milk, and butter in pan. Bring to boil. Remove from heat. Add powdered sugar to make a spreading consistency. Add vanilla or maple flavoring.

*To mistreat God's creation
is to offend the Creator.* 99

Angel Ice Cream Dessert

- 1 angel food cake
- 2 boxes instant vanilla pudding
- 2 cups milk
- 1 quart vanilla ice cream, softened
- 1 3-ounce package strawberry gelatin
- 1 cup hot water
- 1 10-ounce bag frozen strawberries

Break angel food cake into pieces. Put in a 9 x 13-inch glass pan. Mix the pudding, milk, and softened ice cream. Pour over cake. Dissolve gelatin well in 1 cup hot water. Mix in the frozen strawberries; put on top of ice cream mixture. Freeze.

Apple Dumplings

- 2 cups flour
- 2 teaspoons baking powder
- 1 teaspoon salt
- ½ cup shortening
- ½ cup milk
- Half or whole apples, cored

Sauce:
- 2 cups brown sugar
- 2 cups water
- ½ teaspoon cinnamon

Sift together the flour, baking powder, and salt. Add the shortening and blend as for pastry. Add the milk and blend. Pat into a ball, roll out, and cut into squares large enough to cover a half or whole cored apple (pie pastry may also be used). Place half or whole apples on dough squares. Bring corners of dough together at apple top and pinch together. Combine ingredients for sauce. Cook and simmer for 5 minutes. Pour sauce into baking dish. Place apple dumplings on top. Bake at 425°F for 10 minutes, then at 375°F until apples are soft (about 30 minutes).

Bread Pudding

- 2 cups whole milk or half-and-half
- ¼ cup butter
- ⅓ cup brown sugar
- 3 eggs
- 2 teaspoons cinnamon
- ¼ teaspoon ground nutmeg
- 1 teaspoon vanilla extract
- 3 cups bread torn into small pieces (French bread works best)
- ½ cup raisins *(optional)*

Sauce:

- 1 cup whole milk
- 2 tablespoons butter
- ⅓ cup sugar
- 1 teaspoon vanilla extract
- 1 tablespoon flour
- Dash of salt

In a medium saucepan, over medium heat, heat milk just until film forms over top. Combine butter and milk, stirring until butter is melted. Cool to lukewarm. Combine sugar, eggs, cinnamon, nutmeg, and vanilla. Beat with electric mixer at medium speed for 1 minute. Slowly add milk mixture. Place bread in a lightly greased 1½-quart casserole. Sprinkle with raisins if desired. Pour batter over bread. Bake at 350°F for 45–50 minutes or until set. Serve warm.

For sauce, mix everything together and bring to a boil for 3–4 minutes, stirring constantly. Set aside for 5 minutes; pour on warm bread pudding.

Buster Bar Dessert

- 42 Oreo cookies, crushed
- ½ cup butter, melted
- 1 12-ounce jar hot fudge sauce
- 11 ounces salted peanuts *(optional)*
- ½ gallon vanilla ice cream, softened
- 1 9-ounce container whipped topping

Combine cookies and butter. Reserve 1 cup for topping. Put remaining in bottom of 9 x 13-inch pan. Spread ice cream over crust; freeze until firm. Spread warmed fudge sauce over ice cream. If using peanuts, sprinkle over sauce. Put whipped topping over top; sprinkle with remaining crumbs. Freeze. Remove from freezer 10 minutes before serving.

Chocolate Roll

- 5 eggs, separated
- 1 cup powdered sugar
- ¼ cup flour
- ½ teaspoon salt
- 3 tablespoons cocoa
- 1 teaspoon vanilla
- ¼ cup powdered sugar
- 1 quart vanilla ice cream, softened

Beat the egg whites until stiff peaks form. Sift together 1 cup powdered sugar, flour, salt, and cocoa. Beat egg yolks until thick and light colored. Add vanilla and then the dry ingredients. Fold in the egg whites.

Line the bottom and sides of a 10 x 13-inch jelly roll pan with waxed paper. Spread the mixture evenly in the pan. Bake at 350°F for 12–15 minutes or until top of cake springs back when touched; sprinkle with ¼ cup powdered sugar. Immediately invert cake onto clean tea towel; remove from pan. Carefully peel off waxed paper. Don't worry if cake layer breaks; it will hold together when rolled. Starting at one short side, roll up cake and towel together; cool completely on wire rack.

Place roll on tea towel that has been sprinkled with powdered sugar. Unroll cooled cake and spread with 1 quart of softened vanilla ice cream. Roll up cake. Place seam side down, wrap tightly with foil, and freeze.

Cracker Pudding

Mix the first 5 ingredients well. Pour ½ cup cold milk over mixture and let it soak. Heat 2 cups of milk in a double boiler. Stir soaked crackers and other ingredients into hot milk. Cook 15–20 minutes, stirring constantly. Chill.

- ⅔ cup cracker crumbs
- ½ cup sugar
- 1 tablespoon flour
- ½ cup flaked coconut
- ½ teaspoon salt
- 2½ cups milk, divided

Swallowing pride rarely gives you indigestion.

184

Crunchy Ice Cream Dessert

- ⅓ cup butter
- ¾ cup brown sugar
- 2½ cups Rice Chex cereal, crushed
- ½ cup chopped pecans
- ½ cup flaked coconut
- ½ gallon vanilla (or other flavor) ice cream, softened

Melt butter and sugar until blended. Add all the dry ingredients; stir until crumbly. Press crumbs in a 9 x 13-inch pan, saving some for topping. Spoon ice cream on top of crumb mixture in pan. Put remaining crumbs on top of ice cream. Put into freezer until ready to serve.

Fresh Rhubarb Dessert

- 4 cups diced rhubarb
- 1¾ cups sugar
- 1 box yellow cake mix
- 2 cups heavy cream

Mix diced rhubarb and sugar together; let it set for 15 minutes or longer. Prepare cake mix as directed on box. Pour into greased and floured 9 x 13-inch pan. Spread rhubarb mixture over cake batter and pour heavy cream on top. Bake at 350°F for 45 minutes to 1 hour.

Household Hint

Garlic is not only a vegetable, but is also very good for medicinal uses. It aids digestion, relieves dyspepsia and colic, and acts as an intestinal antiseptic and blood purifier. It destroys round and thread worms. It is a good nerve tonic and is very beneficial as a treatment for colds and coughs. It is also very rich in vitamins and minerals.

Old Fashioned Date Pudding

- 1 cup brown sugar
- 1 cup flour
- 1 teaspoon baking soda
- ¼ teaspoon salt
- 1 tablespoon butter, melted
- ½ cup milk
- 2 cups chopped dates, divided
- Whipped cream

Syrup:
- 1 cup brown sugar
- 1½ cups boiling water

Reserve ½ cup dates. Mix all ingredients together. Put in greased 9-inch square pan. Sprinkle reserved dates on top. Combine syrup ingredients. Pour over cake mixture. Bake at 350°F for 30 minutes. Serve with whipped cream.

Strawberry Shortcake

- 2½ cups flour
- 2 teaspoons baking powder
- ½ teaspoon salt
- 1 cup sugar
- 4 eggs
- 4 tablespoons butter, melted
- 1 cup milk
- 1 teaspoon vanilla
- Fresh berries, whipped cream, or milk *(optional)*

Mix together the dry ingredients and set aside. Mix eggs, butter, milk, and vanilla together. Add to dry ingredients and stir together. Pour into a greased 9 x 13-inch pan (or two 8 x 8-inch pans). Bake at 350°F for 30 minutes. Top with fresh berries and whipped cream or milk.

Tapioca Fluff

Serves 12
- 6 cups milk
- 6 tablespoons quick-cooking tapioca
- 1½ cups sugar, divided
- 4 eggs, separated

Heat the milk, tapioca, 1 cup sugar, and egg yolks. When boiling, cook and stir for 5 minutes. Remove from heat and add the egg whites, beaten stiff and sweetened with ½ cup sugar. Stir together for 2 minutes. Pour into serving dishes.

Whoopie Pies

- 4 cups flour
- 2 cups sugar
- 2 teaspoons baking soda
- ½ teaspoon salt
- 1 cup shortening
- 1 cup cocoa
- 2 eggs
- 2 teaspoons vanilla
- 1 cup thick sour milk
- 1 cup cold water

Photo courtesy of Discover Lancaster

Filling:
- 1 egg white, beaten
- 1 tablespoon vanilla or few drops of peppermint extract
- 2 tablespoons flour
- 2 tablespoons milk
- 2 cups powdered sugar (or more as needed)
- ¾ cup vegetable shortening or margarine
- Marshmallow créme (*optional*)

To make the batter, cream together sugar, salt, shortening, vanilla, and eggs. Sift together flour, baking soda, and cocoa. Add this to the first mixture alternately with water and sour milk. Add slightly more flour if milk is not thick. Drop by teaspoons on a cookie sheet. Bake at 400°F. To make filling, beat egg white, powdered sugar, and vanilla. Then add the remaining ingredients. Beat well. A few drops peppermint extract may be used in place of vanilla.

From *Amish Cooking*, published by Pathway Publishers Corporation.

Index